Can
Christ
Become
Good News
Again?

Can Christ Become Good News Again?

By John B. Cobb, Jr.

Chalice Press
St. Louis, Missouri

Library of Congress Cataloging–in–Publication Data

Cobb, John B.
Can Christ become good news again? / by John B. Cobb.
  1. Theology. 2. Cobb, John B. I. Title
  BR85.C543 1991   230   91-31248
  ISBN 0-8272-0456-6

Printed in the United States of America

Contents

Introduction

As a North American Protestant churchman, my greatest hope for the church is for the renewal here of a passionate, progressive Protestant faith. We have seen, quite recently, in the aftermath of Vatican II, a passionate, progressive Catholic faith. Even in its current decline it retains a vitality absent from our Protestant churches in North America. There are still some Protestants old enough to remember the great days of the social gospel, when they participated in a passionate, progressive Protestant faith, and even today there are scattered congregations in which such a faith can be found. That gives me the assurance that renewal of our churches is not impossible.

Meanwhile, nothing is more disheartening than the widespread assumption that only institutionalist, doctrinaire, emotionalist, and legalistic forms of Christianity can evoke passion, that progressive thought waters down Christian conviction and commitment. For one, like myself, who sees institutionalist, doctrinaire, emotionalist, and legalistic forms of Christianity as distortions of biblical faith, and who believes that to be faithful is to be free and open, the present situation of the church is cause for acute pain. Those who rightly demand freedom and openness too often give up on the church, and the institutional church is left more and more in the hands of those who identify Christian faith with one or another of the forms it took in the past.

I long for the church to identify the most pressing problems besetting us, individually and corporately, and to think seriously about the meaning of Christ for these problems. If, as I believe, Christ is truly the savior of the world, then why do we not make that clear in our weekly preaching and our church pronouncements? Why do we continue to describe that from which Christ saves us in such ways that few see the need for such "salvation"? If we convincingly showed how Christ can save us, individually and corporately, from the utterly critical problems we all face, then the church would once again be looked to with expectancy for leadership. There would be authentic excitement among its members. But that would require that we recover the full biblical meaning of salvation, and for that we seem to have no stomach.

Perhaps to be more biblical is too threatening. It would make us aware of the cost of discipleship, a cost many of us are unwilling to pay. It would expose our cherished institutions, doctrines, and rules as crutches many of which faith calls us to relinquish. It would force us to acknowledge that the life of faith lacks the worldly security that we crave and the intellectual and moral security as well. It involves trusting the Spirit when we cannot know in advance where it will blow.

Perhaps the resistance comes equally from having lost the habit of thinking, especially thinking as Christians. To discern how Christ can save us today from the real problems we now face requires thought. As the difficulty of Christian thinking has been recognized, the church has employed professionals to do its thinking for it, but it has paid little attention to what they have said. In any case, the professional thinkers have tended to become an academic community dealing with problems that arise out of the study of the tradition rather than out of its current inner life. Its ministers and bureaucratic leaders are too busy with "practical" matters to engage in profound reflection. So the church grabs at quick fixes, catchy phrases, and public relations gimmicks to resolve the pervasive malaise that all are forced to recognize. The crisis deepens.

If we really believed that the real Christ is the real salvation from the real problems we face, we would not behave as we do. Instead, we would be awed by the challenge so to proclaim Christ and serve Christ that we could guide our society and, indeed, the world away from the precipice toward which it now rushes. To participate in a church that offered the vision of a saved people in a saved world would restore excitement, enthusiasm, and devotion. The church could become again the main agent of God's creative and redemptive work in the world.

If the publication of this book makes any contribution to the renewal of a passionate, progressive Protestant faith in North America, then I will indeed rejoice. Of course, not all the articles here address that need directly, but all of them are written by a Christian theologian wanting to speak to fellow Christians. Collectively they do express how I as a Christian have sought to understand Christ as the real savior of the real world. Even the essay on why I have depended so heavily on the philosophy of Alfred North Whitehead, although addressed to an audience that was not limited to church people, has something of this character.

It is always problematic to gather into a book essays written over an extended period of time. On the one hand, they may not all be consistent. On the other hand, they may be repetitive. I would not have had the courage to propose such a volume. I owe the suggestion to David Polk, who rightly saw that I had addressed the church more directly in scattered essays and speeches than in most of my books.

I owe much more to him. The selection of essays and their organization are his work. The book remains, of course, a collection of essays. But he has given them a sequence and structure that, in my opinion, justify their appearance as a book. I am deeply grateful.

John B. Cobb, Jr.

Part
I

A
Theologian's
Journey

1

Christrist and My Life

I grew up on the "mission field" in Japan. My parents were deeply and sensibly pious. As far back as I can remember, I was conscious of myself as a Christian, not only in the objective sense that my family was Christian, but in the subjective sense that I internalized the desire to be Christian. Indeed, I internalized Christian faith so intensely that I sometimes found my parents' more relaxed and balanced attitudes offensive. I was more self-consciously Christian than most of those who grow up in an ostensibly Christian culture because of my awareness that we Christians were few in number and had a peculiar responsibility to witness to our faith to those who might observe us or talk with us.

This does not mean that I was in fact a good Christian as a child. I was quite inconsistent, vacillating between piety and mild forms of rebellion. Furthermore, being a Christian as I understand it did not fit well with many ordinary childhood experiences. I was often uncomfortable doing things that would have been perfectly wholesome and, on the other hand, at times my natural youthful needs broke through my controls in unattractive and unhealthy ways. There are real problems being too devout too young.

Originally presented at a national meeting of the American Baptist Church in 1974, on the occasion of the launching of its Evangelical Life Style program.

My youthful piety continued in my years at Emory-at-Oxford junior college in Georgia. I joined every religious organization on campus as well as half the others. Not being satisfied with that, I organized a small prayer group with a few friends. We covenanted together to establish strict and ascetic disciplines for ourselves. I spent almost no money and used to send what little allowance I received instead to a mission to lepers in the Sudan. I also went around looking and acting pious in the objectionable sense. Yet, I remember how furious it made me when a cartoon appeared in the school annual depicting me with a halo around my head and an armful of spares hanging from my arm. I fear my piety allowed me very little room for laughing at myself!

As far as I can recall, there was still no dichotomy in my experience between piety and social concern. I remember addressing my fellow students—all too self-righteously, I fear—on the subject of racism in the required chapel. There was much shuffling of feet and accusation of "nigger-lover." But I should add that this did not come from the pious students. The piety I saw in those years was authentic at least in this, both among the students and in the community, that the most devout were also the ones who most fully recognized that racist Southern society was un-Christian. Our little protests in occasionally bringing blacks into the church and dedicating the college annual to the black custodian did no one much good, but they serve in my own memory to oppose the image of the conflict of pietism and social concern.

Of course, I encountered another kind of piety in those years also, often among my own relatives. This was a piety that was the religious expression of the best in the Southern way of life. That way of life included a strong dose of evangelical Christianity; so the piety that expressed it was in many respects Christian. Also, it judged many other aspects of ordinary Southern life as wrong and worked hard at moral improvement. But it seemed to offer no lever for its practitioners to criticize the social order as a whole, which, as was perfectly manifest to all, was racist to the core. This was the dominant form of piety in the churches, and it was only in the circles that practiced a more intense piety that it was broken through. For me, the breakthrough was easy, for I had been brought up in another culture and saw the South first as an outsider. But from this distance, I now rather marvel at how racism had broken through to pious individuals despite its omnipresence and full sanctioning by church and state. I recall also the intense emotional problems of some of those persons who could not reconcile the lives they could not lead in a racist society with their painfully won grasp of the demands of the Christian faith.

So when did I become a Christian? I have never known how to answer that question. Having been baptized as an infant by a Japanese pastor, I joined the church the first year I was in the United States. My parents wanted me to join a Methodist church rather than the union church we attended in Japan, and the minister—after talking with me—probably found I had thought more at the age of seven about what being a Christian meant than had most of his charges at twelve. So there was no problem. But the ceremony meant little to me since, in fact, shortly thereafter we left the church I had joined. As far as I was aware, I had been a Christian before I began to make decisions about it.

Looking back now, I try to appraise the piety of my childhood and youth. I find admirable the dedication it elicited to righteousness and truth as I understood them. I think it also encouraged a healthy self-criticism and the ability to see myself relatively objectively as one among others. But it also led to legalism and its accompanying self-righteousness. I did not understand grace and Christian freedom. Most seriously, it hindered me in coming to terms with my sexuality. I knew that sexuality within marriage was good, but my piety made it more difficult to deal with my actual adolescent sexuality and inhibited healthy development toward maturity.

Shortly after the bombing of Pearl Harbor, I attended a national meeting of the Methodist Student Movement at Urbana, Illinois. The big issue there was whether the Christian should be a pacifist or join the Army. I had not thought a great deal about this up to that time, and I was fairly easily persuaded by the defenders of Christian participation in a just war. Bishop Oxnam was particularly eloquent. Since I spoke some Japanese from having grown up in Japan, I decided to apply for the branch in which I would be trained to serve as a translator, and soon after my eighteenth birthday, I volunteered.

About a year later, when I was stationed at Camp Savage near Minneapolis/St. Paul, I became acquainted with a community of pacifists who were being used as guinea pigs in an experiment on the effects of hunger on human personality. In conversation with them, I discovered that my reasons for choosing military service were not nearly as clear or good as I had thought, and I was persuaded that I had erred in doing so. But I was not quite sure, and I did not know what to do about it. In fact, I was terrified. I sought counsel, but was helped little. The plain fact is that I continued in the course I was in basically out of cowardice.

That taught me something about myself. Up until then I had believed that if I were really convinced something was required by

Christ, I would do it whatever the cost. That was an arrogant and foolhardy belief. It was exposed for me decisively in my inaction at that time. Subsequently, I reverted to the view that participation in just wars is appropriate for the Christian, and I have always believed the war against Hitler was a just one by Christian standards. Hence, I am very glad that I did not go through with whatever I would have had to do to get myself out of the Army or into a stockade. Perhaps Christ used my cowardice to shame my self-righteousness.

Through junior college and the first years as a soldier, I thought that I wanted to be a member of the Government Foreign Service. I was interested in international affairs and believed that this was an area in which Christian commitment was particularly important. I was quite comfortable in this decision, and gave little thought to changing it. But one day when I was stationed at Camp Ritchie, Maryland, all this changed.

I was walking to a Presbyterian church a couple of miles from camp, just across the state boundary in Pennsylvania. In that church I was trying to teach a class of junior high boys on the front row of the sanctuary—quite unsuccessfully, I might add.* Suddenly, I stopped. Out of the blue, it seemed, it had come to me that I should be a minister. There were no reasons. But from that time on, I was quite sure that I would go into some kind of professional ministry at home or abroad. I made little effort to be more specific. But I had little doubt about the direction I was to go.

I will mention a third experience I had in those Army years, quite different from the other two. I continued pious practices during those years, somewhat erratically, but nevertheless quite seriously. These came to something of a climax under the impact of Aldous Huxley. I read his book *The Perennial Philosophy* on a troopship coming back from Japan. Huxley assembles quotations from the classics of all the great religious traditions to support a mystical understanding of God, humanity, and the world. His mysticism seemed to me to be the consistent form of the piety I had consistently practiced. I was deeply moved and fully convinced of the truth of his vision as I understood it. I did not, in fact, become a mystic or even begin serious practice of mystical disciplines. But I did begin to practice the discipline of

---

*Ten years after I made this speech I received a phone call from a Presbyterian minister in Pennsylvania asking whether I was the John Cobb who once taught a class in that church. I confessed that I was. He told me that three of the boys in that class had become ministers and that they attributed their decision in part to my influence. So much for our judgments of "success"!

holding up to God in love and concern the persons who surrounded me. Whether this had anything to do with the experience I want to report, I do not know, but I mention it as one possible partial explanation.

One night I knelt to pray beside my bed in Arlington, Virginia. Before I had consciously thought at all or even collected myself for prayer, I had a vivid sense of spiritual presence. It lasted only a little while, perhaps a minute, and then withdrew. I neither heard nor saw anything. But I will always treasure those moments because in them I knew total acceptance and love.

In 1946, I left the Army and in January 1947 entered the Humanities Division at the University of Chicago. I was still a joiner, and began attending two quite different religious groups. I mention this because I experienced in them for the first time the deep divide between certain kinds of Christian liberalism and Christian conservatism.

At the university student center, called Chapel House, I attended the Methodist student group. I enjoyed it thoroughly and was exposed to all kinds of new ideas and interesting programs and activities. I felt at home and alive, but it did not seem to speak to my more intimate Christian convictions and needs. Accordingly, I began attending also the meetings of the Intervarsity Christian Fellowship. Their intense Bible study and personal sharing attracted me, but I was never quite accepted since I did not subscribe to all the articles of their fundamentalist creed. I felt then and feel today that there is something profoundly wrong when the light-hearted, compassionate, exploratory openness I found in the Methodist group seems to exclude personal piety, and the intense personal devotion I found in Intervarsity is bound up with exclusion, closedness, and reactionary views on most public issues.

After two quarters of bachelor life at Chicago, I was married. Jean and I went for a little while as a couple to both of these groups, but they were otherwise composed of single students and ceased to be appropriate for us. So we looked for a church home and found it at the First Baptist Church. The pastor was Jitsuo Morikawa. I can assure you that neither then nor later did he acquiesce in this unhealthy division of the unity of Christ.

My choice of Chicago stemmed from my experience in the Army. I have mentioned isolated events, but more important than these was the intellectual stimulation of those years. Because I knew a little Japanese from childhood, I entered a unit that was studying the language in preparation for intelligence work. A few students were chosen, like myself, because of having lived in Japan. But most were

Catholic and Jewish intellectuals, many from New York, who saw in this program a more congenial opportunity than in other branches of military service. Through contact with them, I came for the first time to recognize that my southern Methodist piety was only one, quite peculiar, form of religious life, and that indeed Christian faith in general was a highly questionable matter from many points of view. What I heard of Chicago persuaded me it would be a good place to study these modern alternatives to Christianity. I planned first to take a masters degree there in the Humanities Division, investigating specifically all the objections to Christianity, and then to go to a Methodist seminary to get my professional preparation for ministry. But in a few months, I discovered that my understanding of Christianity melted away through my exposure to the thought of the modern world. I was appalled at how quickly a faith I had thought so secure was undercut. I experienced what we have since come to call "the death of God," and it felt very much like my own spiritual death as well.

I knew that there was no point spending three years hammering nails into the coffin of my childhood God. I also suspected that a moderately conservative denominational seminary would not be the place to seek answers to all the new questions that had crowded in upon me. Meanwhile, I had met a few members of the Federated Faculty of the theological schools connected with the university and rightly sensed that the problems that were so terrifying to me were old-hat to them. Hence, I decided to transfer to the University of Chicago Divinity School. There I felt myself drawn into a community of no-holds-barred inquiry centered around the common concern for fresh, contemporary articulation of the Christian faith. That was just what I needed. I continued to take courses in the Humanities Division, especially in the Department of Philosophy, but from that time on, my home was in the Divinity School. In its supportive and accepting atmosphere, I gradually began the long process of putting together a new understanding of God and Christ.

This is not the place to give an account of my intellectual odyssey, yet that has been so central to my Christian experience that I cannot omit it altogether. The destruction of my youthful belief in God had come primarily through a brief exposure to philosophy. I could begin the process of reconstruction only in philosophical terms. Also, I seem to be temperamentally an incorrigible realist and literalist. The question of who and whether God was made sense for me only when approached in a conceptually realistic and literal way. Hence, it was peculiarly fortunate for me that at Chicago I encountered a philosopher who spoke to my need, for, then as now, philosophers who could do so are few and far between. It was Charles Hartshorne to whom I owe the beginnings of a gradual process in which I came again to be able to speak of God with conviction. Through Hartshorne, I encountered the still richer and more complex conceptuality of Alfred North Whitehead, and I have been living with him ever since.

When I left Chicago, I turned to the North Georgia Conference of the Methodist Church for an appointment. I was sent to the Towns County Circuit in the Appalachian Mountains. There I served seven churches while teaching part-time at Young Harris Junior College. I was not a success. The young man who preceded me had built a parsonage for the circuit. His insistence that the toilet be placed inside had split the largest church on the circuit. My task was reconciliation, and at first I made a little progress. But there was folk dancing at a church youth meeting in the neighboring county to which I took a group of our young people, and the church was split again. These were not the battles for which my Chicago education had equipped me, and after a single year, I seized the opportunity to move full time to the Young Harris faculty. After two years there, I went to Emory University and five years later to Claremont.

During the years at Emory and Claremont, I have felt that Christian commitment involves efforts to act responsibly in society. I have engaged sporadically in politics and protest actions that focus on the issues of race and war. The ambiguity of these actions was brought home to me on the one occasion when I engaged in civil disobedience. It was a protest against our role in Vietnam. I was with a large group holding a prayer service in the great public vestibule to the U.S. Capitol. We were shown every courtesy until closing time, but when we continued to sing and pray after that, we were duly warned and then arrested. Our morale was high, supported, I fear, by a good measure of self-righteousness. The next day, while we awaited sentencing, a lawyer came to talk with us. He told us that, depending on the judge, we might be sentenced to six months in jail. Suddenly everything changed. We had felt noble about paying a price of one or two days in prison to witness to our opposition to the war. But we had come assuming that certainly no higher price would be exacted. The idea that we might really have to make major sacrifices for our witness was simply unacceptable! And, of course, we did not have to do so. The judge was very lenient—even complimentary. But the experience highlighted for me the deep involvement of most of us middle-class protesters in the society against which we protested.

The experience focused for me the fact that in these years I have become a part of the establishment, enjoying its benefits, including the freedom to protest within carefully defined limits against the establishment of which I am a part. To a large extent, I have assimilated the values of American middle-class society. I have acquired property and learned to value money. Questions of salary, honoraria, royalties, insurance, and pension funds became important. I found for a few years that the stock market could be an absorbing game. But I have also become increasingly convinced that one cannot serve God and mammon, although the great majority of us middle-class American Christians make a very good try.

The tension between Christ and possessions that I have felt in my adult life has not been as painful as the tension between Christ and sexuality that I felt as a youth. But I believe that it points to a more fundamental issue in the understanding of our faith. This has been too little recognized. We refuse to believe that Christ really calls us to poverty except in that jocular sense in which we all view ourselves as poor in comparison with someone else. Hence, we reinterpret the claim of Christ to be that we should be generous with our surplus wealth—and then often decide that we have little of that. I have always tried to be sure that I give more than a tenth of what I received to the church or worthy causes, and sometimes I have felt quite self-righteous about that, but I don't think I have ever deluded myself into supposing that this is the meaning of subordinating mammon to God. I have tried to decide where to give my time and services somewhat independently of what I receive in exchange, but I have observed that I am quite inconsistent in this, and I often catch myself playing games. Fortunately, in my adult years, I have had a little more ability to laugh at my efforts to be Christian than I had in junior college. So I can admit that I have been divided between God and mammon and hence have served neither one very well. In recent years, it has seemed easier to subordinate mammon much of the time, but I realize that this is because it is also easier to pay the bills than it was once, and because two of my sons are through college and on their own.

It may seem that I am making a great deal out of very little. Surely, it was my first responsibility to take care of my family and get my sons through college, and there was nothing unchristian about trying to earn enough money to take care of them. Indeed, I would have been faithless had I been irresponsible in this matter. So what else could I do? And if there was no alternative, then is it not the part of good Christian sense to enjoy it rather than to beat one's breast?

For me, that argument won't work existentially, although, of course, it did work practically. I have long believed and continue to believe that the deepest apostasy of the Christian church in our society is that it has internalized the values of a capitalist society. We Christians judge the success of persons, including ourselves, very much as the world judges. We have careers in the ministerial profession just as others have careers in business. We are concerned about the rights and prerogatives of our profession just as lawyers and doctors are about theirs. Young people interested in the mission field inquire about travel, educational, and retirement benefits. And why not? We should not regard church vocations as different from other Christian vocations, and certainly we expect laypersons to choose their lines of work according to the rewards. Fortunately, among these rewards, persons schooled in Christian culture are likely to rank the satisfaction of serving others fairly high; so that still plays a role. But surely, this is not quite what is meant by seeking first the kingdom of God.

I suppose that for most Christians, life has always been a tissue of compromises as mine has been. The efforts to produce Christian communities that could be free from such compromises have also had ambiguous results. We have no choice but to accept Christ as our redeemer precisely in the midst of endless ambiguity. But healthy Christianity has at least kept the tension alive in a much more fundamental way than we have done in this last generation. It is simply not sufficient to moralize about the sins of our neighbors in racism or in supporting imperialist ventures while we interiorize the basic values that produce these and other horrors.

At the same time, I have come gradually to understand the meaning of grace and evangelical freedom that, as a professional theologian, I have tried to teach my students. For me to be a Christian is no longer as much a matter of what I do for Christ as of what Christ does for me. One thing Christ does for me, I think, is to laugh at me for taking myself and my beliefs so seriously. Christ laughs especially at my propensity to take a certain pride in my own moral anguish. And because Christ laughs at me, I am released to laugh too, and to enjoy life even in a civilization that hastens to its judgment.

All through the sixties I was aware of a variety of environmental problems and felt strongly about some of them. Who could live in southern California and not be concerned about smog? I was troubled from time to time by reminders that hundreds of millions of people were ill-fed. And I was occasionally distressed by the realization that wilderness was disappearing and with it many of the wild animals that inhabited it. But I believed that technology could solve the problem of automobile exhausts, that goodwill and national generosity could bring adequate living standards to all, and that expansion of parks and reservations could preserve sufficient habitat. I thought that the fundamental ethical and religious issues lay elsewhere: in problems of social justice and international peace.

Illustrative of my general attitudes was my response around 1965 at our Annual Conference to a proposal that the conference take a stand on overpopulation. I had been cynical about the tendency of the conference Board of Social Concerns to bring in a long list of statements on controversial issues on which the conference should act. It seemed to me that we were expected to make pronoucements on the basis of a few minutes' discussion of topics about which we knew very little and on which, in many cases, Christians could reasonably differ. I thought that our assertions were rightly ignored by those in power. When the Board of Social Concerns proposed a resolution on population, I regarded this as a peculiarly egregious case of bringing up a peripheral issue on which there was no reason for us to pass judgment as Christians.

In the summer of 1969, at the urging of one of my sons, I read Paul Ehrlich's *The Population Bomb*. Suddenly the pieces fell together for me, and never again have I thought of world population as a peripheral issue. I saw the interconnection of smog, hunger in Africa, and increasing global population. I saw also that technological solutions by themselves would not work and that goodwill and generosity could contribute to the problem as easily as they could help. I saw that as important as were the issues of peace in Vietnam and justice for minorities in the United States, these must be set in the larger context of the decent survival of the human species. I came almost abruptly to see the task of theology and of Christian ethics in a new light and to form new kinds of political judgments. My professional energies have been partly redirected and my decisions about more personal matters also have been affected. Nevertheless, I can only confess that for the most part I continue to live out of values and assumptions that belong to the world in which I no longer believe, that the changes I have made are utterly trivial in relation to the magnitude and urgency of the problem. For me to achieve personal integrity in relation to my own vivid sense of reality and importance is still agenda for the future. The life that would be involved would be so foreign to the one that I have lived and the one that is lived all about me that I can hardly imagine choosing it.

Let me illustrate. I believe that the planet cannot long support even its present population at anywhere near the present rates of consumption in our country. As a matter of ethical principle, I believe I should not consume more than it would be possible for everyone else to consume. Yet to cut my consumption to the requisite level would be to opt out of American middle-class society, and I do not plan to do that, or even think I should. I am called, rather, to live in the tension between the existing society and the morally normative one.

To detail the little expressions of what this tension has meant in my life is in danger of being both arrogant and petty. However, since we are urged to use our own lives as examples, I will indicate a few gestures I have found it possible to make that are related, however trivially, to my sense of the context in which the Christian life is now to be lived.

We are one of three families that sold our separate homes and jointly purchased a large older one. Especially because of close friendships, we have had a rich year, and look forward to another. At the end of this academic year, one family will move, and we hope to use the occasion to initiate a more self-conscious experiment with new people.* As a family we experimented for one year living without a car. This worked in Honolulu, but in southern California it does not seem practical. Hence, we have bought the least polluting, least consumptive car we could—a Honda. By sharing with another family in our house who has a large, old station wagon, we have been able to be somewhat efficient in our use of gasoline. In my office at school, I have experimented with saving power by neither heating nor cooling the room and by rarely using the lights. Given our mild climate and my large windows, I have found that there is no hardship involved. Where ecological decisions result in fiscal economies, I have passed these along to environmental organizations. I have spent many hours in conferences, committees, task forces, conversations, lectures, writing, and just thinking about the issues.

Of my efforts to date, the fruit that now appears to me most promising is in the life of our School of Theology. With the coming of Dean Freudenberger to our faculty, we have at last the leadership we need to gear our corporate efforts as an institution to address the challenge faced by American Christians as we realize the acute problems of the whole planet and especially the Third World as the revolution of rising expectations crashes head-on into the limits of our ecosystem and material resources. Perhaps as a faculty we can collectively achieve a wisdom that individually we lack. And perhaps we can find ways of making such understanding as we do have effective in local congregations in our region.

---

* We lived in this communal experiment for only four years and then returned to typical middle-class living.

Sometimes I feel that all such efforts are quite useless. Our destiny is being settled by forces of vast scope that no one any longer is able to understand, much less control. Our private crusades, even when magnified by adoption by institutions, appear impotent. Even among idealistic and concerned people, it was the actual shortage of energy that led to turning down thermostats last winter—not the environmentalists' warning of the damage inflicted by our efforts to produce more energy. Similarly, it is likely to be rampant inflation that will finally force us to abandon our habits of waste and luxury rather than Christian principles.

Still, there are reasons for Christians to understand what is happening to them in an inclusive perspective and to learn to evaluate alternatives in global context. Consider our response to inflation as Christian employers and employees. What I have observed thus far is that there is quick agreement in schools and churches that employees should receive increases in salary at least equal to the increase in the cost of living. This is felt as a primary right on the part of the employee and a primary duty on the part of the employer. If this requires that the total staff or faculty must be reduced in size, that price is reluctantly paid.

This means that out of an understandable sense of fair play to employees, Christian institutions, like others, solve the problem of inflation by contributing to unemployment rather than by encouraging less consumptive lifestyles. This can be tolerated because the unemployment is relatively invisible, but overall the result is to widen the gap between the privileged and the unprivileged. If rapid inflation is, as I assume, partly a consequence of limited resources and growing demands, it will probably be with us until basic changes occur in one way or another—an economic collapse, tight governmental controls, or a new economic system. If so, the response by employers and employees alike will either condemn the poor to bear the whole burden or lower the living standards of middle-class professionals like ourselves and unionized labor. What happens at this point may not prove trivial in the long run, and the church could be in the forefront of recognizing the real alternatives, even if the direct economic power of its decisions is minor.

I ask myself whether we professional church people, if we were persuaded of the accuracy of this analysis, would elect to allow inflation to cut away our economic status. I am not optimistic, but I still do not think that the effort to instill new attitudes is worthless.

I see the situation as somewhat analogous to that in the South before the civil rights struggle. Here and there were individual whites who refused to accept the Southern segregation mores. They were admirable but ineffectual. There was virtually no chance that they could change established patterns, and, in fact, they had to compromise all the time in order to survive and to have a context in which to speak and act. The change came only when it was demanded vociferously by the oppressed and by their allies in other parts of the country where no personal price had to be paid for this particular form of morality. Nevertheless, I am convinced that the Christian conscience of many conservative white Southerners had a great deal to do with the ultimate outcome. If they had been genuinely convinced of the rightness of the cause of segregation, they would have thrown their support to the forces of blind resistance rather than obey the new laws. The Ku Klux Klan would have grown a hundredfold. Nothing short of an army of occupation could have forced open the segregated facilities or saved from mass murder the blacks who led the protests.

Resistance did not go to these lengths, first and foremost, I believe, because we white Southerners in large numbers knew that there was something morally indefensible about our way of life. We were not prepared to change it voluntarily, and we resisted change in many ways. But there were limits to our resistance, and more and more of us, with a certain inner relief, began to cooperate with the new system.

Our present middle-class defense of our economic status is quite analogous to the earlier Southern white defense of the status quo. Like that, it condemns others to make sacrifices so that we will not have to change our ways. We have lots of goodwill for the Third World and the poor within our own country, but we do not acknowledge that our basic values and lifestyle are contributing to their problem. Most of us can still defend with great complacency our need for cost-of-living raises in our monthly paychecks. As long as we are morally secure in this defense, and as long as the disadvantaged do not see what is occurring, there is little likelihood of change. Once the moral issue becomes clear, we will still resist change that would require our sharing the sacrifices with the poor, but our resistance will become halfhearted. The Christian conscience can soften us up for needed change even if it is too weak to lead to its voluntary acceptance.

One reason for the long resistance of Southern white Christians to basic change in racial patterns was that we could hardly imagine what successful integration would be like. We could not picture our children in integrated schools or worshiping in integrated congregations. When we tried to do so, we were repelled, and stories of racial troubles in Northern cities did nothing to allay anxieties.

Similarly, today, as middle-class American Christians, we find ourselves unable to imagine how we could live on half our present real income. We consider the cost of maintaining a home and a car and sending our children to college, and even at our present economic levels, we find this difficult. We will no more voluntarily choose to deny our children a college education than would we Southern white Christians voluntarily choose to send our children to integrated schools. But the fact that some measure of integration was working reasonably well in some parts of the North at least complicated the picture for the Southern white. We now need vivid images of a good life that is economically much less costly than that to which we are accustomed in order to introduce a comparable complexity into the consciousness of middle-class Christians.

It is at this point that more fully committed Christians can make important contributions. They can seek out creative ideas about new lifestyles appropriate to the times into which we are moving and experiment with some of them. They can develop a variety of models one or another of which may be sufficiently attractive to persons clinging to their present security as to give them the courage to act upon conscience. Even a few thousand people prepared to experiment with such lifestyles might affect the national climate sufficiently to make the transition to less consumptive lifestyles far smoother. Let us hope that out of its tens of millions of members, the American churches can find the requisite thousands.

Consider first a modest experiment. A local congregation could gather a half dozen families who covenanted together to undertake to keep their dollar expenditures constant in spite of inflation. They would agree to share with each other their progress and the methods they employed. As the cost of operating automobiles rises, they can purchase smaller and more efficient ones, walk where they were in the habit of riding, manage on one car instead of two while cooperating with neighbors, enter car pools, and so forth. As the cost of utilities increases, they can turn down their thermostats in winter, do without air conditioning in summer, and cut by half their use of electric lights. Homes could be better insulated, and the more adventurous might experiment with solar heat. As the cost of appliances rises, they can manage with fewer. As the cost of clothing goes up, they can learn that style is not as important as they once thought, and that there is no reason a woman should feel humiliated by wearing the same attractive dress repeatedly. As food prices continue to rise, the consumption of meat could be greatly reduced. Costs of a child at college might be partly offset by moving into a smaller place or renting out a room. Vacations might be planned as camping trips nearer home.

Some families would find this adventure fun. Some, whose dollar income continued to rise while they kept expenses steady, might be willing to give what they had saved to one or another of the all too urgent causes that seek help from us all. By sharing with the congregation and community what they were doing, those in the experiment would be spared part of the embarrassment that the economies would otherwise cause. And I suspect that others in the community would have their habits modified too. Persons who had experienced this possibility themselves or had observed it in others could move hopefully into a future that others dread and resist.

As economies cut out the obvious fat in our affluent lifestyles and ways of further economizing become matters of real hardship, participants in such groups would increasingly realize that our society has turned what should be luxuries into necessities. The private automobile is the most important case in point. Even for families that work hard at economies, it usually represents at least $1,000 a year in costs, and this minimum figure is rising rapidly. Persons may also realize that much of the cost of the goods they buy pays for waste. For example, a factory uses great quantities of water to cool its equipment and then pumps the water back into the river, often seriously damaging the ecosystem. Meanwhile, in our homes we use energy to heat the cold water that flows through our pipes. If the factory were not so far away from our homes, the heated water they waste could provide us with hot water and heat our homes in winter to boot. Similarly, the great cost in time and energy of collecting our wastes makes recycling so costly as to save but little. How much better we could live on how much less if our cities were constructed differently!

I am convinced that Paolo Soleri has thought through these and related questions far ahead of the rest of us. He offers us in his arcologies the context of a new style of life both far more rewarding than most of us now know and far less costly to the biosphere. Consciousness raising about the difficulties of economizing in our present cities may lift to the necessary height the demand for a quite different type of city. If so, it will have performed an important service.

If middle-class people grew accustomed to a less expensive style of life, both church and state might be able to improve their ministries to the disadvantaged as well as to increase their staffing of educational institutions. But for the foreseeable future, needs for such ministries will outrun funds available at an accelerating rate. The trend of the past few years will continue, with needs increasing while both church and state withdraw. There is no real shortage of persons willing and qualified to engage in the requisite social services, but there seem to be no channels through which they can do so.

Such a situation calls for some Christian ingenuity as well as commitment. New lifestyles can be devised that will address themselves to these needs. I will sketch the one that occurs to me as a model worthy of exploration.

Suppose five families were concerned about the very high rate of recidivism among ex-convicts and believed that a Christian ministry to those newly released from jail was of great importance. They might decide that a center should be set up where such persons would be welcomed, helped to adjust to society, and given an opportunity to participate in a warm and accepting Christian community. Or suppose these families were concerned by the absence of effective Christian witness and ministry on a university campus. They might decide that a new style of chaplaincy and personal service program was needed. Suppose they felt that the operation of one of these centers would require three full-time persons. They could turn to the church, but few churches at present are looking for new projects of this sort to finance. Alternately, they could decide to do the job themselves. That would involve pooling resources. Together they would have to find the funds (through selling their present real estate, for example) to purchase facilities both for them to live in and for the center. Second, they would have to decide how many incomes they needed to support both their families and the center. Perhaps four of the highest earners in the group would agree to continue their present employment and support the whole undertaking. Perhaps three other adults would make child care and housekeeping their joint responsibility. That would then free three adults to serve in the center, calling on the others for specific help as needed.

There is clear evidence that such a community can endure through any substantial period of time only if each participant is self-consciously committed to Christ and willing to confess that faith. General goodwill does not survive the hard knocks of communal living or the repeated failures and conflicts that would inevitably characterize the shared effort. Again and again, individuals would have to re-examine the grounds of their involvement in the undertaking—and if, among all the complex of motivations, devotion to the suffering servant were not at the center, they would find excellent reasons to withdraw. Devotion to Christ requires continual expression and sharing if it is to have the strength to withstand the inevitable strains. The community cannot last long without worship.

At the same time, it is very important that the devotion be truly to the living Christ and not to a rigid or legalistic principle. "Christ" is too often named in defense of some cause or conviction dear to the heart of the speaker. When "Christ" is thus employed, faith in "Christ" divides one from other believers and prevents the open, learning, sharing, questing relationship to which the living Christ calls us. The worship that can unite and hold together such a community will be one of continual renewal of dedication to a call that transcends every particular goal and purpose of the group or its members.

If the strains and tensions are overcome or endured through Christian love, the rewards of such sharing of life and service can be immense. Perhaps the most important will be the sense that one can integrate one's life in interdependence with others around Christ. That is an experience few have today with comparable wholeness.

I have spoken of conscious commitment to Christ expressed and renewed in worship. But the theme of evangelistic lifestyles raises another question as well. Does serving Christ in community call others to Christ explicitly? Should it try to convert to Christ the ex-convicts or university students it serves?

My assumption is that the answer to these questions is affirmative. If Christ has a clear, dominant meaning in one's life, if that meaning is the focus of love and the ground of being loved, if one believes that what one experiences with Christ others can experience too, there is no reason for reticence. But we should not ask Christians to speak beyond their clear, assured convictions—as has so often happened. Nor should the name of Christ be spoken in such a way that our favors are conditional on the response. Among the gifts Christians have to offer, the greatest is knowledge of Christ.

Like all their gifts, they offer this one when the time is ripe and when they sense readiness to receive. In the context of an inclusive evangelistic lifestyle, those occasions will be far more frequent than when, as for most of us, our basic life decisions are largely governed by aims at security and success that are in conflict with Christ.

I have suggested two kinds of Christian community that are possible today and relevant to the world into which we are being drawn. Of course, many of us will not find the opportunity to participate in either. Our calling may be a more lonely one. The sharing that we find possible may be much more fragmentary. I do not disparage that kind of commitment. It is the most difficult of all.

But I am addressing you as leaders of the Christian church in the United States. The norm for the church is not that it place an enormous burden on each of its members to struggle in painful isolation to find the way. The norm is rather that the church provide a context in which each strengthens the other and shares with the other. I once thought of myself as a strong individual who could hew to the right whether others approved or not. I have found that I deceived myself. I can go only a very short distance by myself. Beyond that, I need the approval and support of friends.

It is too much to ask of a local congregation that as a whole it constitute a community of encouragement of radical experimentation. But it is not too much to ask that it support within it groups of persons who can help one another to move forward. Yet, even that is very rare.

I believe that in the years immediately ahead, there will be increasing recognition that our society cannot go on indefinitely along the lines it has followed. There will be willingness to listen to ideas that seemed outrageous to most people a few years ago. But there will be impatience with pious generalities when solutions are so urgent. Of all the major institutions of our society—government, education, medicine, industry, civic associations, labor unions, and the church—it is the church, with all its weaknesses, that will have the best chance to give creative leadership. For a long time, we have not dared to propose radically Christian solutions to problems even in operation of our own institutions because they seemed so unrealistic. But in the years ahead, the discontinuity between our proposals and socially accepted practices need not deter us. Only radical solutions will be practical. Even the teachings of Jesus will seem relevant. Persons of genuine commitment who live out their professed convictions will be heard.

If we do not offer solutions that are hopeful and possible for a free society, it is likely that our free society will erode rapidly. Our chance to speak to the pressing issues of the day may be lost for a long time. I congratulate the American Baptist Convention for its serious approach to the present opportunity.

2

Why Whitehead?

The title "Why Whitehead?" has been chosen for these remarks partly because there is a slight alliterative element in the title. But it is also a question to which many people want to know the answer. I am not going to argue against other choices, because one can make a good case for giving a lot of attention to other people. But out of my personal experience with the thought of Alfred North Whitehead, I would like to explain why he has become an increasingly important resource for me and why I have become increasingly convinced that Whitehead's thought has value and usefulness for other people as well. Though I will be going through a sequence of answers to the question "Why Whitehead?" in terms of my own experience, I think that I reflect in most of these points something much wider in our culture than just my own private experience. I take the opportunity to be biographical on the assumption that this is also part of the history of this generation.

The story begins for me at the University of Chicago. I had heard Whitehead's name before, when I was in the Army. But I had it mixed up with Leslie Weatherhead, and when people talked about Whitehead, I thought it was Weatherhead. It was not until just before

Delivered at the annual banquet of the Center for Process Studies, Claremont, California, October 19, 1979.

I got to the Divinity School at Chicago that the name began to take on some meaning for me. Because many people have read the book *Zen and the Art of Motorcycle Maintenance,* I am going to begin by saying what I was doing at Chicago before I went into the Divinity School. I was a student in an interdisciplinary program in the Humanities Division called "The Analysis of Ideas and the Study of Method." This is the same program that the author of *Zen and the Art of Motorcycle Maintenance* took, and the professor under whom I took the most courses is the same professor who drove the writer crazy. This was quite literally true in his case, and it had a considerable effect on me too. I kept going back and taking more courses with him because I hadn't been able to figure out what was going on, and it was very tantalizing to try.

In the meantime, while I was very confused about what I was learning, I was also having a religiously and existentially important experience. The religious faith with which I had come to Chicago no longer seemed to fit the kind of world to which I was being exposed in the graduate program. I do not mean by this that there was some particular argument that was terribly persuasive, that proved why I could not believe something that I had formerly believed. It was simply an experience of not fitting. The God whom I had grown up believing in just did not fit in with the world as I came to understand it. The whole thing fell apart for me.

It was during that time that what little I began to hear about Whitehead seemed to promise a different way of putting things together. The difference was not just a matter of a different way of thinking of God, though that was certainly involved. It was also a different way of thinking of the world. And so, without quite knowing what was going on, I found myself particularly attracted to Professor Charles Hartshorne. He was teaching at Chicago and through him I became acquainted with Whitehead's thought. I also learned from other professors in the Divinity School who talked about Whitehead. But they seemed to mean something quite different from what Hartshorne was talking about. I found this fascinating and confusing. Rather than simply adopting what I was being specifically taught either by Hartshorne or by the Divinity School professors, I felt an increasing need to get acquainted with the thinker they were all talking about but who seemed to be different from any of them. In any case, in my own experience, as for a good many process theologians, the first reason for being interested in Whitehead was a religious interest. He seemed to offer a way of dealing with the intellectual and cultural system of the modern world, genuinely appropriating it, but also going beyond it so as to overcome its nontheistic or even atheist tendencies.

God and Power

I will indicate just one problem that many Christians have found to be very acute. One of the main reasons why people have found it difficult to believe in God is that the kind of God they have believed in does not fit with the kind and quantity of the evil in the world. This is a traditional problem that people have been wrestling with for many, many centuries. How can we believe that the source, the ground, the creator of the world is good when we see so much cruelty, injustice, brutality, perversity, and deceit in the world that this God is supposed to have created?

The way in which Whitehead has understood God and God's relation to the world and the nature of the world enables us to affirm the goodness of God in relationship to the world without the kinds of paradoxes and strange distortions that have come into so many doctrines. Whitehead has provided for us a way of understanding God's power that is different from the usual images of power in the Western tradition. His understanding of God is, indeed, quite new. It has basis in scripture, and when one looks to the tradition, one can find it in many places. But it has not dominated the way God has been thought of in the tradition.

Let me briefly indicate the difference. Usually, when people speak of one being as powerful in relation to other beings, they seem to think of the ability to compel or to force the other beings. I have power over a pen in the sense that I can pick it up and the pen has nothing to say about it. I can make the pen go up and I can drop it. The pen has only a very slight power to resist. It has weight, and that is power to resist, but I can overpower that power. This ability to overpower other beings has, to a large extent, been thought of as the kind of power that God has. But if God has the power to overpower everything else and make everything else do exactly as God wants, then it is very difficult to understand why there is so much sin, suffering, misery, and destruction in the world.

Whitehead had a different model for understanding power. Power in general, and God's power in particular, is the ability to persuade. I am trying to persuade you here. I am exercising some power. I am presenting ideas and I am hoping that some of those ideas will commend themselves to you. But I don't think anyone is being forced to accept anything. You are, I hope, being appealed to in terms of your freedom. If I can present ideas to you that are a little different from ideas that you have had before, then, rather than overpowering you or forcing something on you, what I'm doing is expanding your freedom. You are free to think something you weren't previously free to think—and you are also free to reject it. You have a widened range of freedom. The power to expand the freedom of other people is very different from the power to overpower other people and compel or force them to do something that you have predicted that you want done. Whitehead thought that both kinds of power exist in the world, but that the more ultimate power, the greater power, the more fundamental power, is the power to give life and freedom to others rather than the power to force others to do one's will—to overpower others in that sense.

The problem of evil—that is, of understanding evil in the world—is a very different kind of problem when one thinks of divine power in this way. Of course, evil is still a problem. Evil doesn't go away because you think about it and think about the ways of dealing with it differently. But with a different view of divine power, the problem that has been dealt with through most of Christian history takes on a different shape. The Center for Process Studies is planning a conference with a Jewish group that has asked that we focus on the problem of the Holocaust. You may know how doubly painful the Holocaust has been in Jewish experience. First, there has been the actual and still incomprehensible suffering of six million Jews through systematic, intentional destruction. That is a very special kind of evil carried out with advanced bureaucratic and scientific methods. The failure of the rest of us to do anything to prevent it from happening is also a part of that evil.

Then there is the second evil. That is, there is the evil that in light of the Holocaust it becomes extremely difficult for the survivors to believe in God because in Jewish history our God is the Lord of history. One understands God in relationship to historical events. The God who allowed the Holocaust is, in stronger terms, a God who caused the Holocaust. If God makes everything happen the way it happens, God is responsible for the Holocaust. How can a Jew believe in such a God anymore? So there has been a struggle among Jewish thinkers over how to deal with this double victory of Hitler: first, the destruction of millions of Jews and then the threat to Jewish faith. The problem of evil is the underlying problem, and some Jewish thinkers have felt that perhaps process theology can be of some help in trying to understand God and how God works in history in a different way. We hope that our conference will encourage people to pursue that kind of interest. This contribution to thinking about God and evil is one of the reasons for "Why Whitehead?" It is the most narrowly and specifically theological reason.

The Fragmentation of Contemporary Thought

The second reason is also a religious reason, but not perhaps as narrowly theological a reason, because one way of understanding the meaning of religion is in terms of binding things together. Religion is a way in which the totality of things can be organized and ordered so as to make sense of life and of the world. In our modern world, such unity as our ancestors had has broken down into fragments. We have multiplied the number of academic disciplines, and this isn't just a matter of the university. It is also a matter of our professional skills and the kinds of communities into which we are segregated as life goes on. Each one of us can understand only one little piece of the totality. We have lost the sense that our little piece belongs to a larger whole that makes some sense out of the little pieces. You could say there is no longer a university; there is only a multiplicity of separate disciplines that for political and economic reasons will meet in adjacent rooms and adjacent buildings on campuses. The deepest division is the division between the natural sciences and the humanities. We have become accustomed to speaking of the two cultures: the culture that is oriented to the natural sciences and the culture that is oriented to the humanities. There has been a lot written on how difficult it is to communicate across those lines.

Part of the problem is that we know too much. Nobody can possibly know everything, and so it is more convenient to divide knowledge up and have a lot of specialists. But another reason for the problem is that modern philosophy has given up the effort, even the purpose, of attempting to put it all together, and a way has been worked out for dividing up things. The biggest divide was, of course, the divide between nature and history. That divide took place in the work of the greatest philosophers near the end of the eighteenth century, and it has structured the very understanding of a curriculum in the university. This philosophical divide has certainly encouraged the great division in the university and, beyond that, so many other divisions. Also, on the cutting edge of physics, the most prestigious of all the sciences, there has been a sense of the breakdown of any possibility of thinking things together. Many people in other areas, when one talks about the possibility of a coherent vision of things or some way of understanding the totality of life, point out that we now believe one cannot have a consistent view even within the area of physics. If one cannot have a consistent view even in the area of physics, how could one expect to put *everything* together into a coherent view?

The most famous expression of this in physics involves relativity theory and quantum mechanics. Physicists haven't been able to put these two together. These two major frontier disciplines in the most prestigious of natural sciences use mutually contradictory patterns of thinking in order to develop their scientific formulae. Even within quantum mechanics, one finds that for certain purposes we say that the ultimate units of reality are waves, and for certain other purposes we say they are particles. Finally, it just depends on what one wants to do at the time as to whether one proceeds as if the world is made up of waves or of particles. These are simply illustrations of the way in which the sense of an objective, unified reality has broken down in the twentieth century. Even the effort to put things together is quickly dismissed in many circles as showing that one has not gotten past the eighteenth century. It is assumed that anyone who understood the nineteenth century would not press for such a unified vision.

The cultural consequences of this fragmentation of knowledge are very serious in our time. I will indicate one specific area in which I think they are serious (one could point to many others). This takes us again to the area of our religious life.

The Christian faith through many centuries gave people a sense of living in a world that made some kind of sense. There was some appeal to people to live appropriately to the way things really are, and to do this in all areas of their life because all the areas of their life fit into this single vision. The church could be seen as an expression of wisdom and understanding that gave meaning at the same time it fed upon all the specific elements of knowledge that could be gleaned from many sources. A church like that can be healthy in its contribution to society. But, sociologically and intellectually speaking, as time has gone by, we in the church have bit off a smaller and smaller portion of the pie as being the area in which we have something to say. Sociologically speaking, we are largely reduced to dealing with the family. We don't even know how to deal with single people very well. We now find only the very private and inward elements of life appropriate to deal with in the context of Christian faith.

Intellectually, we have supposed that Christian faith belongs on the side of the humanities rather than the natural sciences. Then we go through the humanities and find out that faith belongs to one very special discipline, usually the interpretation of one particular element in our literary heritage. So we end up with theology as one academic discipline among others, dealing with little more than the interpretation of the Bible. That is a tremendous restriction, and it is not surprising that when the church understands itself in this way, it is restricted to a smaller and smaller ghetto in the total life of the modern world. It is not even very sure what the importance of that little sliver is anymore, because of the deep demoralization of the church that has resulted from the last two hundred years of intellectual and cultural life. There remains a certain kind of hunger on the part of people that then cannot be satisfied in that limited context.

One of the reasons for the vast new interest in astrology and the emergence of all sorts of cults in our society is that they pretend to put everything together for people. They do so in terribly simplistic ways that are not capable of withstanding much criticism from the side of any one of these fragmented disciplines. But the disciplines are so fragmented that none of them any longer have much authority. One can just wrap up oneself in a form of religious thinking that is intellectually irresponsible. We could say all sorts of negative things about this, but who can blame such a person? We need unity. We need some kind of wholeness to give shape to our lives, and our major traditions are not able to do that anymore. I think that is a very high price to have paid for having bought into this fragmentation.

Whitehead is the one major thinker of the twentieth century who has really tried to put things together. To do that, one has to know mathematics, physics, biology, physiology, psychology, history, and religion. Whitehead was not an expert in all of these. But he had enough depth of knowledge at enough points that his was a serious undertaking to think more deeply in each area until he could find a point of unity. This involved a fundamentally different way of understanding the nature of reality, one that makes it possible to build up a new coherent vision. One has to think past waves and particles to a different notion of what the physicist is dealing with and, at the same time, one has to think in a different way about human existence, to name only two examples. This takes radical reconceptualization, and no one else in the twentieth century, as far as I know, has done this in a sufficiently revolutionary and comprehensive way to be a serious alternative to Whitehead.

Of course, other people have proposed holistic visions. I have mentioned some of the cult leaders of the sixties. They provide holistic visions too. But they leave out all the details; the visions fail to hold up when the details are brought to bear. There are others who have done good jobs within some limits. Teilhard de Chardin did a very good job, but he did nothing with mathematics, physics, or chemistry. These are rather large omissions if one really wants to bring all things together. Our culture needs to be saved from fragmentation. The Christian community needs to be saved from it, since the fragmentation renders it increasingly irrelevant. It is truly important that we explore the possibilities Whitehead offers and test the adequacy of the direction in which he pointed.

Let me hasten to add that Whitehead would be the last person to say, "I have now got it all straight, all you have to do is memorize what I said." He understood his effort as being in a sequence of efforts that would need to be superseded by others. Very few people seem to have caught up with him yet, so superseding will take a little longer. I hope that the next generation will be genuine superseders.

Ecology

There is a close relation between ecological concern and overcoming fragmentation. But I did not make that connection until ten years ago. I had already been angry about smog, so concern about particular environmental problems was not new. But suddenly, I saw that one problem in relationship to a lot of other problems. I saw the world in a whole new perspective that changed my way of evaluating what I and other people were doing. It was a conversion of sufficient radicality that I was prepared to re-examine the basic philosophical and theological beliefs that I had held prior to that time. But what happened to me was not that I felt led to reject Whitehead. Instead, I came to have a deeper appreciation of his vision.

One reason that the ecological problems could get so serious before many people in our society paid any attention to them was that the way in which our intellectual life had been structured meant that we just were not able to look at the whole. Each one of us had a particular angle. Economists looked at matters in one way, biologists looked at matters in another way, engineers looked at matters in still another way. Nobody looked at them in an inclusive way. This was particularly important among theologians, who have been among the slowest to understand the nature of the problem. We have been taught for generations to separate history and nature and see that Christian faith had only to do with history and did not have to do with nature. We assumed that nature took care of itself, that the physical scientists dealt with that, and that it was none of our concern. If you think nature is outside the horizon that Christian theologians are supposed to deal with, you do not pay close attention to it. And you do not allow what you see to have much effect upon the content of your other reflections. One of the reasons we had let things go so far was precisely the kind of fragmentation and division that Whitehead had been devoted to overcoming.

At first, I was surprised that Whitehead had not done more with this problem. Then I discovered that he had. But when I had read his works earlier, I had had other interests and just skipped over the relevant passages. I realized the same thing was true of my teacher, Charles Hartshorne. There were many passages in his writings that dealt explicitly with environmental problems, but until I became interested in them for another reason, I just passed over them. I came very late to recognize the relevance of this particular intellectual tradition.

Another relevant element in both Teilhard and Whitehead is the conviction that all things have some kind of inwardness or subjectivity. All things are centers of experience and not simply objects for the experience of others. If one really views the totality of nature as, in this sense, "alive," then the incongruence between viewing things as alive and seeing that we treat them as if they were inanimate or dead begins to disturb us and forces us to readjust our thinking. The sharpest contrast comes here between what a Whiteheadian or a Teilhardian sees and thinks when approaching an animal and what someone who is most influenced by Descartes believes. Descartes explicitly taught that animals are only machines and that their shrieking or crying is no different than noises emitted by machines that are not properly oiled. Most common sense never went along with Descartes. But our economic theory did go along with Descartes. Animals have become simply resources whose value is judged completely in economic terms. Our ethics went along with this because our Christian ethics never taught us that we should worry about animals. Humane societies had to develop almost *against* the opposition of the leading Christian ethicists of the time. The Pope refused to allow a humane society to be organized in Rome because he thought it was not Christian to be concerned about the way animals were treated.

In our Western tradition, we accepted an understanding of the other creatures on the planet as mere objects. Ecological sensitivity is heightened when we stop objectifying other living things and appreciate them. Whitehead can help us make that change.

Feminism

Another challenge in the past decade, which none of us who taught in theological schools could have avoided even if we had tried, has been the new issues raised by women. This has not occurred only in the theological context, but I think it has been especially emphasized there. I came late to all of these things. Feminism had not been a topic of major interest to Whitehead, but we were pleased to turn up a speech that Whitehead made during the time that women's suffrage was an issue. He took a strong stand in favor of women's suffrage based upon his own philosophical principles. Hartshorne had also been a lifelong feminist in every self-conscious way. But none of that had dented my horizons of thinking at all until I was forced to attend to it by daily contact with women who were insisting that the status of women is a matter of utmost importance.

Many of the issues that women have been raising are related to the kinds of topics of which I have been speaking. For example, we find a great deal of feeling on the part of feminist Christians that the traditional Christian doctrine of God expressed a very one-sided and biased masculine emphasis. By the "traditional" doctrine, I do not refer as much to the Bible as to the doctrine that has been worked out over the centuries, especially by philosophical theologians. There is not only a question of language—always male language about God—but also of the content and the substance of the doctrine of God.

Let us take the very central theological doctrine that because God never changes, God cannot be affected by anything that happens. That is not a biblical doctrine by any stretch of the imagination. But it certainly played an enormous role in Christian theology from the second century well into the twentieth century. It also reflects and supports the view that the best situation for a human being is to be impervious to being affected by others. That is a caricature of a masculine stereotype. And if we think of God in that way, this certainly is going to have an effect upon the whole range of our religious life. Whitehead, though not with feminist issues consciously in view at all, has provided us with an extremely different view of God as one who is perfectly affected by everything that takes place. The one idea of perfection is to be totally unaffected by anything. The other idea of perfection is to be perfectly affected. I think the latter is a more Christian doctrine for various reasons, including its correction of the excessive one-sidedness of the masculine domination of concepts and images. In any case, it is an idea that Whitehead had taught me for philosophical reasons long before I knew it had anything to do with masculinity and femininity.

My point in all this is to say that these important challenges which required serious reconsideration at many levels for me nevertheless did not have the effect of weakening my commitment to Whitehead. Of course, there are many strong feminists today who are so critical of every form of inherent philosophy and theology that they are not going to adopt any of the patterns that have already begun to be developed by men. But among those women across the country who are concerned to be feminist Christians, Whitehead's thought has had more positive resonance than that of any other male thinker. We were able to hold a conference at Harvard—organized, of course, by the women at Harvard—on process theology and feminist theology. It was a successful conference. Many women theologians participated. Not all fully accepted Whitehead. But the conference was an occasion for testing the rich potentiality of this tradition in that whole range of concerns with which we will be struggling for another fifty years at least.

Christianity and Buddhism

For me, the seventies also have been the time of intensification of interest in the question of the relation of Western and Eastern thinking. Western thinking is very much bound up with the Christian faith. I am also convinced that Eastern thinking needs to be approached through specific Eastern traditions, not through some abstraction that might be called Eastern thinking. The approach I have followed is through Buddhism, and especially Mahayana Buddhism. The Buddhist-Christian dialogue is not the only way one can take hold of the East-West relationship, but it is one good way of considering it.

I have found that the encounter with Buddhism has both reinforced my interest in Whitehead and led me to read Whitehead in ways that I had not perceived him before. The same was true, of course, of the encounters with feminism and environmental thought. In the Buddhist case, it went more deeply into the metaphysics itself. One of the startling features of Whitehead's theological reflection was that he declared that God was not the ultimate. Of course, in the Western tradition, we have always supposed that God is the ultimate. The word *Being* has been taken as virtually synonymous with God in the mainline of traditional philosophical theology. Whitehead's statement could be reformulated to say God is not Being itself. This is in sharp contrast with Paul Tillich, who said that God is Being itself. That is a properly debated issue in modern theology.

It is interesting that those who have most understood themselves to be biblical theologians rather than philosophical theologians have all along been very critical of the idea that God could be identified as Being itself. They had generally supposed that if you went the philosophical route, you would have to say that God is identical to Being itself. Many of them have used this as a reason for rejecting philosophy. Emil Brunner is one who has stated these things most unequivocally, and he probably shaped the form of "neo-orthodoxy" in the United States more than any other one thinker. Whitehead, on strictly philosophical grounds, came to the same conclusions that many biblical theologians have arrived at on biblical grounds, namely that this identification of God with the metaphysically ultimate reality—Being—is a mistake.

Whitehead doesn't use the word *Being*; he uses *creativity*. Creativity is his way of talking about the metaphysical ultimate. By the metaphysical ultimate, he means "that of which all things are ultimately constituted." The easiest way to suggest what kind of a question this is an attempt to answer is in terms of physics. When we analyze the nature of a thing, whether it is a table or a book or anything else, we come down to smaller and smaller physical units. We used to think that when we got down to atoms, we had come to the end. Now we know we're just beginning when we get to atoms, and have several steps more to go. Still, somewhere along the way, one comes to the end of the kinds of things that can be characterized, that is, that have some kind of form or shape. An electron has characteristics that differentiate it from a photon, but what is it that they both have in common? They are both units of matter-energy; at least that is one way physicists might talk about them. But matter-energy is really more "energy" than "matter." What electrons and photons have in common is that they are both embodiments of energy. What differentiates them can be discussed in terms of such things as frequency, mass, spin, and electrical charge.

The philosophical question is, then, "What is this of which all things are ultimately composed?" It has no form or character of its own. Still, we use some kind of word to name it. In most traditional Western philosophy, we would say it is Being. I have proposed that it is labeled by physicists as matter-energy or just energy. Whitehead calls it creativity. Thus, creativity has no form of its own. Creativity is equally and in an identical way embodied in an electron and in a human experience, because both are expressions of creativity, and creativity as such is neutral with respect to all of its expressions or embodiments. To call that *God* does have some effect upon the whole direction of religious concern and attention. But when it is called God in the Western tradition, there is a strong tendency to attribute to it some characteristics that really do not belong. Paul Tillich would say that his characterization of Being itself is all symbolic language. Still, it seems that he means some of those symbols rather seriously, although the metaphysics does not justify this. Whitehead says there is another reality, quite different from creativity, which is the ground or the principle or the source of freedom, of novelty, of order, of the increase of value. That is a very different kind of principle from creativity or Being itself.

The distinction that Whitehead made was one with which many process theologians have been uncomfortable. I struggled with it in the book I wrote in 1965.* Hartshorne just ignored it and worked out his system in a different way. But when I began reading Buddhism, I discovered that the Buddhists were talking about very much this kind of an ultimate. They would never call it Being, because the term *Being* tends to connote that it is something solid—something that is really there, something one can lean on. They say, quite the contrary: It is not Being, it is Nothing. It is empty of all being. There is no substance there at all. It is precisely this emptiness, this chaos, this nothingness or formlessness, that is ultimate. One can, through intense meditative disciplines, realize that one really and truly is an instance of this formlessness and this emptiness, and that all the forms and shapes and special characteristics do not really characterize the ultimate. They do not characterize what I truly am. This statement, by using the word *I*, is already a very misleading expression. No form can characterize what is as it is because, of course, it is not! One is forced to use paradoxical language. But the breakthrough, what constitutes enlightenment, is the existential realization of this nothingness or this emptiness. Then one ceases to impose forms in the world and simply lets things be what they are.

When I came to understand increasingly what it was that Buddhist scholars were talking about, I recognized it as what Whitehead was talking about when he spoke of creativity. This is something very different from what Whitehead was talking about when he spoke of God. What he was talking about when he was speaking of God was much more like Yahweh than it was like the void out of which, from which, Yahweh created. *Void* is a good term for the ultimate reality of Buddhism. This seemed to be a way of understanding the relationship of two great religious traditions that no longer presented them as two ways of talking about the same thing or as two handles on the same reality. What one comes to know and to be through Buddhist discipline is something that we in the West have only very remotely and tangentially approached. Meister Eckhart is the favorite Western mystic thinker of both Hindus and Buddhists. He seems more of a Hindu than he is a Buddhist. But the Buddhists like him too, and he certainly comes close to their understanding. He made the distinction between Godhead and God. Whereas God has a formed character, Godhead is beyond all form.

A Christian Natural Theology.

Quite to my surprise, a distinction that Whitehead had come to on strictly philosophical grounds turned out to be rich and fruitful for interreligious understanding. Whitehead knew that Buddhism was very important. He thought that Christianity, Buddhism, and science were the three most important movements in the world today. He said that Christianity and Buddhism are both in decay, and will continue to decay until they mutually learn from one another and also from science. Since the time he wrote, science also has begun to decay. I think science will also continue its decay until it is prepared to learn from Christianity and Buddhism. But Whitehead may be able to help us bring these three great movements of the human spirit into mutually fructifying and enriching relationships. Perhaps out of that there can be some hope for a new birth of civilization.

3

Theology: From an Enlightenment Discipline to Global Christian Thinking

What is theology? That question has become less important to me in recent years. At the same time, I have not ceased to reflect on what is most important for me to do, as a Christian enabled by the church to spend time in thought. I have concluded that insofar as "theology" is the name of an academic discipline (*Wissenschaft*) confined to a particular method and subject matter, it is not worthy of the amount of attention it receives—little as that truly is in our time. Indeed, I have concluded that academic disciplines in general are today more the problem to be overcome than suitable contexts for Christian vocation. They have ceased to be effective channels of the quest for wisdom and have instead become self-preoccupied islands of refined information. The truly urgent questions fall outside the province of any discipline or combination of disciplines—including theology as a discipline.

What I do feel called to do is to think, self-consciously as a Christian, about those important questions to whose answering I have reason to hope I can make some contribution. Prior to the Enlightenment, this is what was meant by "theology," and in a post-disciplinary world, I hope "theology" can mean this again. So I

Previously published in German translation in Johannes B. Bauer, ed., *Entwürfe der Theologie*. Vienna, Austria:Verlag Styria, 1985.

continue to think of myself as a theologian—though not as a systematic theologian or a dogmatician.

God as Christ

The most important of all questions, now more than ever, is the question of God. Apart from belief in God, I see no basis for hope or grounds for judging anything to be really important. Apart from belief in God, I would have no reason for opposing the fragmentation of knowledge into self-contained disciplines. Thus, belief in God is presupposed in everything I do or say or think. But that by no means sets this belief apart from others as one not to be doubted and challenged. On the contrary, because I believe in God, I find it supremely important to reconsider and to doubt my belief. Also, because God is of ultimate importance, how we think of God deeply affects how we live. Every misunderstanding of God reflects itself in misdirection of human energy.

For me, rightly to understand God is to understand God in and as Christ. I know that there are those who apprehend the same God in other ways, and I rejoice in that. But my own belief in God is not separable from Jesus Christ. My concern is not about some "ultimate" in general but about that which was incarnate in Jesus. I believe that what was incarnate in Jesus is present or incarnate also as the life of all living things and as the light of understanding in all people (John 1:4). I try to discern how that life and light are present in my own life and throughout the world. I try to trust it, letting go of the false securities to which I am inclined to cling. This divine presence in all creatures, that was incarnate in Jesus, I experience as creative and transformative, and so I have called it creative transformation.* This creative transformation I also call Christ. Because I believe in the actual, immediate, redemptive working of Christ in the world, I have hope that the human race will be guided around the multiple catastrophes toward which it is heading.

I have hope. I do not have certainty. I observe *how* Christ works in me and in the world. Christ is the giver of life to all who live, of freedom to all who are free, of understanding to all who understand, of love to all who love. Apart from Christ, there could be no life, no reason, no imagination, no personal or social redemption. Christ's power is incomprehensibly great. But nether in Jesus, nor elsewhere, does Christ compel human beings to respond to the divine gift, promise, and call. Christ does not act as one agent alongside others, but in the empowering and directing of every agent. If we human

---

* I have developed this theme in *Christ in a Pluralistic Age.* The Westminster Press, 1975.

- Creative trans.   - initial aim.
- primordial
- holy spirit

beings punch the buttons that launch the nuclear bombs, Christ will not prevent them from destroying the earth.

If we allow ourselves to be drawn by Christ away from this suicidal sacrilege, and yet we continue to rape the earth, pollute the air, poison the waters, and melt the polar ice caps, Christ will not block the self-destructive consequences of our action. It is Christ who warns us, stimulates our imagination to consider other ways to order society, and calls us to make peace with the rest of creation. Apart from Christ, there would be no hope. But there can be no assurance that we will attend to Christ's call.

Christ and Judaism

This Christocentric faith might seem to lead toward lack of appreciation for other religious traditions. But for faith in "Christ" to lead to exclusivism and the rejection of others is to turn Christ into an idol. One of the important questions for our time is how to open ourselves to others and to learn from them as Christ calls us to do. Because of the particularly vicious behavior of Christians toward Jews over many centuries, it is especially important that Christocentrism not give even the appearance of anti-Judaism or be used to affirm the supersession of Judaism by Christianity.

For us who believe in Christ as the Power of God incarnate in Jesus, there can be no doubt that Christ is found throughout the history of Israel and Judaism. There is also no doubt that Christ was known, attested to, and served. But of course, "Christ" is not the name by which Jews have known what we know as Christ. Indeed, Christ is not the only name used by Christians either. We speak also, especially, of the Holy Spirit. One name appearing in the Jewish scriptures and available for use by Jews and Christians alike is *Sophia* or wisdom. She played in Jewish rhetoric a role much like that of *Logos* or Word in John's prologue. Indeed, it is just as appropriate to think of Jesus as the incarnation of the Wisdom of God as the Word of God. Apart from John's prologue, the New Testament gives equal support to this usage. I will return to this later.

It is through Jesus that we Christians have been engrafted into that community that has lived most fully in and through its history with the Sophia of God. By such engrafting, we came to share the faith and promise by which the Jewish community also continues to live. The tragic history of over-againstness between Christians and Jews has denied to Christians much of the potential richness to which our engrafting should have made us heirs. It has also led the Jewish community as a whole to disown its finest son and thus to be impoverished in its turn. We may hope that the day is now dawning when both Christians and Jews can find wholeness as the gift of Jesus through the present working of Christ.

Christ and Buddha

Whereas it is evident that Jews and Christians, along with Muslims, have unity in the worship of one and the same God, despite significant differences of language and concept, there are others who do not share this unity. Christians have much too quickly condemned them as pantheists, polytheists, and atheists. But Christ leads us beyond judgment to listening. When we listen, we find in many of them also the wisdom we seek and serve. Especially fascinating to Christians are those Buddhist traditions—the major ones—that oppose all forms of theism and yet produce saints and monastic communities as impressive as any in the Christian heritage. What does it mean to believe in God and live by God's saving Word and Wisdom when it appears that others find profound fulfillment by turning away from all that these names designate? Can one continue to speak of Christ as the one hope of all the world in the face of a Zen master?

Many Christians, puzzled and troubled by these questions, seek in the Buddhist's language the equivalent of "God," even though Buddhists deny any interest in God and urge that salvation requires us to surrender all clinging, both to that idea of God and any reality it is supposed to designate. These Christians often think they are aided in their quest by the apophatic tradition in Christian mysticism in which the true God, or the Godhead, is approached through negations and known as beyond all possible conceptualization. But there is a problem here. If that which is found in apophatic mysticism is not appropriately trusted and worshiped, it is not the God of the Bible. If it is appropriately trusted and worshiped, it is not the Nothingness, Emptiness, or Emptying that is realized through Buddhist meditation.

My proposal is that we recognize that Christ is not the same as Emptying, and that we listen and learn from the Buddhist about the profound reality and salvific meaning of the realization of Emptying. We can learn from Buddhist history how those who have truly become empty have been filled with wisdom and with compassion for all sentient creatures. Why should we resist the truth of a tradition older than our own through which so many have found so much?

Yet, there is a mystery here for the Christian. If Christ is the life and light of all people, obviously Christ is present throughout the Buddhist community and especially in its sages and saints. Then how can it be that they have directed attention elsewhere and often criticized every effort to name the power of life and light?

What we learn from our encounter with Buddhism is that God's way with human beings is far richer, far more complex, than we had thought. In order to live abundantly, it has seemed to us that we should learn to discern Christ—to be trustingly responsive to Christ's prompting or call. This has had its enviable effects. But Buddhists learned a different truth. They found that every concept became a screen blocking people from the true actuality. Concepts of the divine are particularly pernicious because they seem so important. People should not only cease clinging to their ideas and meanings; they should also avoid holding fast to a reality beyond the concepts. The need is to let go completely. This cannot be done if one clings to the idea of a result to be expected from letting go or even to the idea or reality of letting go. What is required is beyond any exercise of the will, but there are disciplines, utterly simple yet painstakingly difficult, that lead toward the final letting go or emptying.

Buddhists are hesitant to describe the condition that results from Emptying, but they agree that it is one of wisdom and compassion. It is also a condition of fullness. When one lets go of everything, one is then filled with everything—only now it is everything as it actually is, not as it is fitted to our hopes, fears, and memories. And when this happens, when actuality as it is fills one, there is perfect blessedness of Buddhahood.

It is here that Christians discern Christ and at the same time recognize how much their own hopes and fears and memories do in fact block the working of Christ in their lives, preventing the gift they can see in the Buddhist saint. Christ, unknown, unnamed, and unsought, floods into the heart of the Empty One as Christ cannot do in those who, while trying to discern and trust Christ, yet remain full of themselves. To say that Christ is the one hope of the world is not to say that *believing* in Christ is the one hope of the world, important though such believing is.

There is another side of Buddhism and another witness to Christ to be found there. Although Christians cannot but marvel at the authenticity of the Zen master and the other Buddhist saints, one must also note, in all honesty, how few they are among the whole Buddhist population and how remote Enlightenment seems to the masses of Buddhists. This does not deny that ordinary Buddhists are affected—and positively affected—by the Buddhist ideal. But it has meant that many Buddhists have despaired of ever approaching Buddhahood. Pure Land Buddhism arose to meet their need.

One of the major forms of Pure Land Buddhism in Japan is Jōdōshinshu. It is based on the radical judgment that the quest for Buddhahood through difficult disciplines is futile and misguided. Shinran, its thirteenth-century founder, taught that human beings are fundamentally sinful and have no capacity to save themselves by spiritual disciplines or in any other way. Their only hope is trust in Other Power for their salvation. This Other Power is Amida, who is totally gracious and ready to give both the needed faith and the salvation that faith brings. Millions of Buddhists through faith have found life in the grace of Amida.

The history of the idea of Amida is profoundly different from that of Christ, and the content of the two ideas also differs. Yet Christians can hardly doubt that the gracious Wisdom they know and experience as Christ is known and experienced also in Jōdōshinshu, and in other forms of Pure Land Buddhism, as Amida.*

Recovering the Present Reality of God

I find myself drawn by Christ into the meeting with Jews and Buddhists and others. In the course of those meetings, I must surrender the way I have previously thought of Christ precisely for the sake of knowing Christ better. Christocentricity and universality do not conflict. If it is truly Christ who is the center, there can be no boundaries.

I have spoken of this matter at some length, because how we think of God is supremely important. Unfortunately, being what we are, we humans incline to idolatry. People associate God with one culture, one religious tradition, even one set of values and customs. We Christians must confess with shame that we have not been, and are not, free from idolatry. Nevertheless, in principle, to know God as incarnate in Jesus—to know God as Christ—can break the hold of idolatry upon us. Nothing is more important than that.

Some Christians, in their zeal to avoid idolatry, have erred in another way. To avoid associating God with any creaturely limitation, to avoid placing any limit whatsoever upon God, they have stressed the divine transcendence. When this is carried all the way, it becomes impossible, in any straightforward sense, to affirm God's presence in the creaturely world. Of course, these Christians are correct that God transcends the world. There are depths and heights in God that lie far beyond all that we can say and think. But the one-

---

* I have discussed the relation of Christianity and Buddhism in *Beyond Dialogue: Toward a Mutual Transformation of Buddhism and Christianity*. Fortress Press, 1982.

sided emphasis on transcendence prevents one from accepting the scriptural vision of God as genuinely, redemptively, present and active in creation. It makes a mockery of incarnation, or else it so separates the incarnation in Jesus from God's relation to all else that the incarnation loses continuity with living Christian experience. Christocentrism then becomes a Jesus-centeredness that cannot avoid Jesusolatry. Too many Christians accept the post-Christian vision of the absence of God and adopt the practical atheism that separates compartmentalized modern knowledge from faith in God. Faith becomes a leap in the dark, a relation to one-knows-not-what, rather than a trust in the God who is in us and with us as Christ.

The account of the absence of God can be a profound adaptation to the world brought into being by the Enlightenment, a world that systematically built a wall to keep God out. We must be grateful to those who have refused to abandon their faith in God even as they were drawn deeply into this Godless world. Their subtle paradoxes have made Christianity possible for other sensitive people despite the profoundly alien intellectual context. I do not wish to condemn them in any way. In them, too, I see Christ.

But this self-enclosed world of the Enlightenment is not the biblical world, and its foundations and underpinnings in science and philosophy have already crumbled. The autonomous world hangs on chiefly in the scholarly disciplines it produced, disciplines that often fail to reflect on their own foundations because they have none that can withstand examination. Dogmatism, no longer as common in the churches, is almost universal in the academic disciplines. The most creative thinkers in every field have long since abandoned the academic disciplinary structures and reopened the questions these have tried to foreclose. Why should Christians continue to take so seriously this Enlightenment world from which God was excluded? Can we not identify God again in the life and light and freedom and love that no disciplines ever succeeded in explaining away—however hard they tried?

However, to understand the world in a genuinely post-Enlightenment way is not an easy matter. It requires rethinking all the issues considered in the formation of the Enlightenment synthesis and proposing different answers. These must be tested in relation to the vast knowledge gained in the Enlightenment period, and then must also be examined in their relevance to the data that the Enlightenment disciplines cannot encompass. We cannot simply will the demise of the Enlightenment worldview with its resultant fragmentation of knowledge. We must create a new unified vision based on a different model of reality.

This kind of activity falls outside the *discipline* of theology. Indeed, like so much that is needed, it falls outside all the disciplines. But if theology is self-conscious Christian thinking about important matters, few projects could be more appropriate for theology.

There are many, even many Christians, who suppose that in dealing with such questions one should set aside one's Christian identity in order to be objective and neutral. This attitude reflects the victory of the Enlightenment and its penetration into the church. Faith is understood as something special, appropriate, if at all, only in a separate sphere of religious inquiry. But I could not be a Christian if I did not believe that there really is a power that gives life and light by giving itself— in short, if I did not believe in the reality of Christ. Since I do believe in Christ and that I am called by Christ to understand all things in relation to Christ, I *must* seek an understanding of the true nature of all things as a Christian. To do so self-consciously serves as a check against prejudice and distortion. It is not a distorting bias to be set aside for the sake of objectivity.

Replacing the Atomistic Model

As a matter of biography, I would not have the courage to participate in such a project apart from the influence upon me of the thought of Alfred North Whitehead.* He made the one great attempt in our century to develop a post-Enlightenment cosmology that deals seriously with the conclusions of the physical sciences as well as with religious experience. That cosmology was incomplete, and the passage of half a century has brought much new knowledge requiring integration. Adjustments must be made. But in general outlines, and often in surprising detail, Whitehead's speculations continue to be illuminating and unifying. They offer a model of reality quite opposed to the Enlightenment one and better able to interpret the wide range of data. This mode, which I now call "ecological," has become a part of the way I perceive and think. It has influenced everything I have said thus far and will affect all the rest. It will be useful to describe a few of its salient features in their contrast with the central Enlightenment model, i.e., atomism.

Ordinary language refers naturally to two kinds of things: objects and events. One speaks of a tree or a star, on the one hand, and of a fire or a meeting, on the other. Both are readily understood. But beginning with these two notions, ontological inquiry asks how they

---

*Whitehead's most important book is *Process and Reality*. Corrected edition by David Ray Griffin and Donald W. Sherburne. Free Press, 1978.

are related. Modern "common sense" assumes that objects are fundamental and that events happen to objects. The *wood* burns and *people* meet. The objects are primary, the events, secondary. Indo-European languages encourage this assumption.

To explain the events, then, one analyzes them into objects and their relations one to another. It is changes in these relations that constitute events. Further, these relations cannot really affect the objects in question, for if they did, events would alter objects, and objects could not explain the events. The only real relations among objects must be external to the objects. They can, in fact, be only spatial. Objects can change in their spatial relations to one another without being affected by these changes. Hence, the final vision is of unchanging material objects in relative motion.

Obviously, this vision would make no sense if we took our initial commonsense objects as examples. The wood changes when it burns. It becomes something quite different, such as ashes and smoke. So this vision of the primacy of objects over events does not speak directly of the objects of common sense. They obviously change in ways other than relative spatial location! Instead, this model refers to a quite different type of object—one that is indivisible and hence indestructible—the atom.

This model always created conceptual problems, and it was never verified. The original reasons for accepting it were a mixture of philosophical, political, and religious ones. It was not needed for physical science and indeed was not held by most of the first generation of modern scientists. Nevertheless, it won the day and dominates, or lies in the background of, almost all Enlightenment science.

Although the model never succeeded in explaining all the data even of physics, its most acute and dramatic problems have appeared in the past century. Verbally, at least, a problem was created by the discovery that what had been identified as the atom was not a true atom, but this could be resolved by seeking the ontological atom in subatomic "particles." The real difficulty began then. The subatomic world simply does not yield to explanation in terms of indivisible and indestructible, unchanging particles in relative motion.

Since the entire atomic hypothesis hinges on there being such ontological atoms, this discovery of their nonexistence is a decisive refutation. But by the time the refutation became indisputable, the sciences were established as separate disciplines. These were all founded on the atomic model, and of course they all had vast success at the level of detail. Hence, most branches of physics, along with chemistry and biology, continue to operate on a model that has now been proven false. Those practitioners who reflect on the assumptions of their disciplines usually think that acting as if this false model were true is essential to their continued progress.

The Ecological Model and Its Implications

Whitehead proposed that we follow the other option of taking events as fundamental and understanding objects as composed of events. Of course, here, too, the theory does not apply immediately to objects of common sense. We are asking most directly and obviously about the ultimate indivisible entities that make up the physical world, the subatomic entities. Whitehead believed that the "particles" found there can be better understood as successions of events rather than as indestructible and unchanging atoms. He believed further that the wave-particle duality can be resolved if we think of a field of events.

It might seem, on first glance, that it matters little to our overall worldview whether the subatomic world is composed of objects or events. But this is to misunderstand. If events cannot be explained in terms of matter in motion in the subatomic world, then there is no reason to suppose that they should be explained in this way in the ordinary world either. This alters the nature of scientific investigation throughout. I will offer an example. Consider physiological psychology. Its basic program has been to explain human experience in terms of brain physiology. It may speak of "events" in the brain in the process of this explanation, but the underlying assumption is that such events are themselves products of matter in motion. Physiological psychologists do not expect to carry the explanation through to the end, but their whole program is reductionistic.

The evidence, of course, has never verified the reduction. Superficially, all would agree that there *appears* to be an influence of human decisions on the brain as well as of neuronal changes on human experience. But in the orthodoxy of the discipline, one direction of explanation is taken to be scientific, the other, not. Hence, there is no systematic examination of the influence of free human decisions on the brain comparable to the study of the reverse influence. Fortunately, the evidence for two-way influence is so strong that there are a few "heretics," including at least two winners of Nobel prizes. Still, their dissident voices have not changed the program of the discipline.

But if events are ultimately more fundamental than objects, then there is no reason for the reductionistic bias. It is more appropriate to consider the subject matter of physiological psychology as the interaction of innumerable events including human experiences. Nothing that has been learned in the reductionistic Enlightenment discipline need be denied, but the conceptuality through which the information is ordered will be changed, and whole new areas of investigation will complement the reductionistic ones.

The difference of the event model and the object model can be brought out through a feature of events not yet mentioned. In contrast to the atomistic model, the relations among whose units can only be external, events are richly related internally. They do not change relative spatial positions as do atoms, because they do not move at all. But the occurrence of one event grows out of the other events that make up its environment of its world. These other events are internal to it. Hence, the real things that make up the world are not separable from their environments. In a different environment, there would be a different event. The event-model is a relational model or an ecological one.

Enlightenment science, shaped by the atomic model, makes the opposite assumption. To investigate scientifically is to remove a thing from its ordinary environment and examine it in an artificial one. Animals are put in laboratories in order to examine behavior under controlled conditions. There they are cut into pieces so that their behavior can be explained by the functioning of their organs and glands. No doubt, much has been learned by this reductionist method. But the Whiteheadian model would lead one to expect that an animal's behavior in a laboratory is quite different from its behavior in the world, and the organ's functioning when removed from the animal is quite different from its functioning in the living body. It would encourage more field study and less vivisection as a way to learn more important facts about the animal. But the pressure of established disciplines founded on the atomic model still cuts against this type of inquiry as "unscientific." Even ecologists are pressed to move away from the examination of the concrete interconnectedness of things in the actual world to mathematical models they can study on computers.

Adoption of the ecological model would end the dualism of nature and history, of mind and matter. It is true that many people already deny that they are dualists. But as long as the disciplines within which they work assume atomism in their self-definitions as well as in their structure, methods, and goals, the whole weight of "knowledge" will be to fasten dualism upon human thinking. Private objections will have little effect in the public world. Only if the most prestigious models of inquiry come to be based on the recognition that there is no human experience that is not bodily through and through, and no event in the body in which human experience is not a constitutive factor, will the power of the dualism of mind and body be broken. Since this human microcosm is only an illustration of a pattern than extends everywhere, all the disciplines will need to be replaced by new organizations of knowledge. All events are constituted by their relations, and these relations cut across the artificial disciplinary boundaries. The ecological reality should be reflected in the structures of thought and investigation.

The model of relational events applies also to the relations of God and the world. Neither exists in itself and then enters (or fails to enter) into relation with the other. God participates in the occurrence of every creaturely event, and God shares with every event all that it becomes. God's perfection consists not in self-contained completeness but in complete inclusion of the world. God is the supreme example of the ecological model.

Some object that by giving so large a role in my thought to a model learned from a modern thinker I have subordinated the Bible to something alien. I do not agree. I know no one who does not think and interpret the Bible in terms of some notion about reality, consciously or not. Most, today, are deeply influenced by the Enlightenment model, even if—indeed, especially if—they have never thought much about it. This model is deeply antithetical to the biblical worldview and has seriously weakened our living relation to the Bible, whereas Whitehead's model is far more continuous and congenial.

The ecological model is not found in the Bible. But the accent there, too, falls on events more than on objects, and its understanding of reality gives a large role to relations. The dualism of humanity and nature, of mind and body, is alien to the Bible, as is any notion of a self-enclosed world from which God is ordinarily or always excluded. The division of knowledge into disciplines and sub-disciplines whose explanatory methods systematically exclude God's action is equally remote to the biblical vision. Of course, that vision is prescientific, and Whitehead's is not. I have no interest in defending all aspects of the biblical worldview—nor Whitehead's either, for that matter. But whereas the hermeneutic of the scholar of an Enlightenment discipline has required radical excision of the "valid" biblical message from the biblical worldview, a Whiteheadian hermeneutic allows for a less fragmented appropriation.

The Social Location of Theology

Thus far in these pages, the context in which I have spoken of God has been the religious-cultural-scientific one. What happens in this sphere is important for the future of humankind. I do not apologize. But gradually, beginning about fifteen years ago, I have come to realize the one-sidedness of this approach. It takes seriously the cutting edge of Western intellectual development, but it pays too little attention to the suffering of the poor. It locates Christ in life, light, freedom, and love, but it ignores questions of justice and revolution. I have never been personally indifferent to human suffering and injustice. I have understood my concern for all human beings as a fundamental expression of Christian identity. But for many years, I thought that Christian reflection on the questions of the relief of suffering and oppression belonged to the discipline of theological ethics and not to that of systematic theology. It took years of buffeting by black theology, liberation theology, political theology, and feminism before I was fully aware of the seriousness of this distortion. But I do now understand that oppression is a theological problem as much as an ethical one*—or, more accurately, that this distinction of theology and ethics is a disastrous part of the heritage of the disciplinary organization of thought, one by which I myself had been particularly victimized.

I reluctantly accepted what was for me the new issue of my own social location as explanatory of my theological work. This was difficult. Thinking in terms of social location seemed *ad hominem* and reductionistic. It was often posed in such a way as to imply that everything I had done as a white, middle-class, North American, male university professor was automatically invalidated. I did not believe, and do not now believe, that to be true. I could see, as I have already noted, that the structure of disciplines in the seminary had blinded me to important questions and that some of my more strictly academic work had little justification outside the priorities of my discipline. But where I had been guided by genuine religious concern, and by concern for the human future, I resented the pejorative implications of the sociological account.

Nevertheless, I was forced to acknowledge that my work was white, North American, middle class, and male in ways that I came to regret. I *had* allowed the problems I posed to be shaped by the understanding of Christ in the white church without reflecting on how questionable such an understanding must be in view of the association of that understanding over a period of centuries with the enslavement and degradation of blacks. I *had* allowed myself to be directed in my inquiry by the issues troubling Christians in the North

---

* See James Cone, *The God of the Oppressed*. Seabury Press, 1975.

American middle class and remained almost oblivious in my theological reflection to the far more urgent concerns of most of humanity. And I *had* traced history and interpreted Christianity in terms of the elite male experience. I have still not dealt adequately with these matters, but they are now part of my horizon as I think self-consciously as a Christian. They force me once again to doubt my understanding of Christ.

By identifying Christ with creative transformation, I had been led to focus on the history of spirit in a way analogous to Hegel.* This directed attention to the times and places where cultural and intellectual breakthroughs occurred. The comments above on Judaism and Buddhism reflect this focus.

I had attended also to the work of creative transformation in individual existence. And here I had seen a point of contact with one motif of liberation theology developed by Paulo Freire.** Conscientization impressed me as a powerful account of the work of Christ. As late as the early seventies, when I wrote *Christ in a Pluralistic Age,* I saw Christ in the conscientization of the poor, but I did not see Christ in the poor themselves except insofar as I saw Christ in all.

I was dissatisfied, but I did not find, at first, a way to go further. Christ is the incarnation of the Logos, which is the creative and redemptive work of God in the world. How can one discern that as distinctively present among those in whom what is often apparent is exclusion from the effective working of this power? I did not question that God loves the poor, that their lives, like all lives, are precious to God, or that we are all called by Christ especially to serve the poor through conscientization and in other ways, since it is they who can profit most from such service. But I could not then, and cannot now, associate the Logos with a special identification with the poor. It is not as Word addressed to us but as Lover who suffers with us that God identifies especially with the poor.

But was that Lover of the world just as fully incarnate in Jesus as was the Word? What else could it mean that Jesus said that what we do "to the least of these" we have done also to the one who is our ultimate judge (Matt. 25:40)? Indeed, it has been through Jesus that Christians have learned the lesson, already taught by the prophets to Israel, that God identifies with the oppressed rather than with the oppressor.

The problem for me was that I had followed the tradition of the church in holding that only one person of the Trinity, the Logos, was

---

* As in *The Structure of Christian Existence.* Westminster Press, 1967.
** Paulo Freire, *The Pedagogy of the Oppressed,* tr. by Myral Bergman Ramos. Herder, 1970.

incarnate in Jesus. I had then been too bound by the connotations of that term. I had not taken with sufficient seriousness the church's teaching of "the exchange of idioms" through which all that belongs to each person belongs to all. I had understood Jesus from the point of view of what was incarnate in him rather than determining what was incarnate in him from Jesus.

I am trying to learn better. I would like to go one step beyond the church's traditional teaching. That tradition, in addition to unifying the Trinity through the exchange of idioms, declared that in all actions in the world, *with one exception*, all persons of the Trinity co-acted. Hence, it does not ultimately matter whether we speak of God's redemptive activity in the world as Father, Son, or Spirit. But the church did make the one exception, and that was the incarnation. According to official teaching, only one person was incarnate in Jesus.

To me, now, perhaps in too impatient a reaction to my earlier too slavish adoption of this restriction, the restriction itself seems *ad hoc* and undesirable. Is not God's Spirit incarnate in Jesus as much as God's Word? What is gained by denying this? In the context of the early church's debates, some justification—at least some explanation—can be found, but today such distinctions complicate, and too easily distort (as in my own case), Christological thinking. In Jesus we find incarnate not only the creative, directive, and redemptive activity of God, but God's suffering love as well. "Christ" names all of this. It is for this reason it is profoundly true that what we do to the poor and the oppressed, we do also to Christ—for it is particularly in them that we see and meet Christ.

There is another way in which I have learned to identify Christ with the poor. Christ is also the truth. Previously, I had understood this in terms of the creative transformation of thought and had seen it especially in the great intellectuals and artists. I did not really appropriate the idea that the truth is to be found in the foolish of this world, although I did not want to reject this biblical paradox (1 Cor. 1:18–31). I was eventually forced to acknowledge that through my own attention to the "wisdom of this world," I had failed to recognize the social location of that wisdom and had been blinded to much of the deeper truth of the human situation. That truth I had learned from those who spoke from the perspective of the poor and the oppressed. The wisdom of the oppressors diverts attention from this oppression. The foolishness of the oppressed recognizes it for what it is and explains also the obscurantism of the oppressors. It is in the foolishness of the oppressed that Christ as truth is found.

Christ is the incarnation of God's suffering love and God's truth as much as of God's creative and transforming activity. Recognizing this prepared me to accept *Sophia* or Wisdom as the primary and most adequate name for that which is incarnate in Jesus. In the passage in which Paul speaks of the falseness of worldly wisdom, he also names Christ as the Wisdom of God. The rich meaning of Wisdom in Jewish and Christian thought, its association with justice for the poor and God's love for the world as well as God's work in the world, have all been taught to me by another oppressed group—women.* To understand Jesus as the incarnation of Sophia breaks the monopoly of masculine images in Christian thought about God, and as one lives into this Jewish image, one finds that not merely linguistically, but also connotatively, Wisdom is both richer and more feminine than either Word or Spirit. To think of God as Christ and Christ as Sophia is both in continuity with our scripture and liberating for both men and women. It means that Christ is no longer simply "he." Christ is also "she." By living into old images that are new for most Christians, we also can break the stranglehold of masculine language in our liturgies.

These changes in Christology seem to be appropriate expresses of what I have been taught by the various liberation theologies. They are not mere rhetorical adjustments. For a Christian, how one thinks of Christ determines how one understands one's world and to what one attends. The need to change is always with us, and Christ draws us into new experience and new understanding.

In Pursuit of Global Theology

One difficulty is that there is no ready way to respond to all the challenges at once. In the process of responding to feminist concerns, the problems raised by black and liberation theologians often are not only neglected but rendered more difficult to solve. Even more apparent is that the changes called for by blacks and Latin Americans often fail to address the concerns of women. Meanwhile, I have been increasingly aware of the ecological crisis, the threat of nuclear destruction, the increasing tribalization and idolatry everywhere, the curse of Christian anti-Judaism, and the profound wisdom of primal peoples. In the midst of all this, how can one who continues to be white, North American, middle class, and male play a responsible role? The only answer I can find is that I must strive for a global theology, that is, one based on as inclusive an understanding of the global situation as possible.**

---

*The fullest discussion to date is in Elizabeth Schüssler Fiorenza, *In Memory of Her*. Crossroads, 1983, pp. 130–140.

**Although the need for global theology may be particularly acute for North Atlantic white males, it is felt by others as well. See the book of the Sri Lankan, Tina Balasuriya, *Planetary Theology*. Orbis Books, 1984.

To base one's thinking on the global situation does not mean that one always speaks about it. Comprehensive description and overview has its place. But what is needed now equally is to discuss many different topics with this global situation in view. Each of us needs to identify those areas in which our own experience and abilities allow us to make a contribution to the radical re-thinking that is needed on all subjects. In concluding, I will describe some of those projects that I have been led to undertake by this understanding of the theological task.

The first book of global theology to which I contributed was *The Liberation of Life: From the Cell to the Community.** My co-author was the Australian ecologist Charles Birch, who has long been a leader in the Church and Society subunit of the World Council of Churches. He, too, has been deeply influenced by Whitehead's thought. We shared the conviction that the World Council commitment to a just, participatory, and sustainable society is a sound one and that it can be given more substance and force when set in the context of a total ecological vision. We are both convinced that as long as practical decisions are directed by specialists or experts from established disciplines, there will be no movement at once toward justice and toward sustainability. A different mindset is needed. We developed the ecological model and displayed its relevance for the understanding of all life, including human life, and the implications of this way of understanding life for technological, economic, and other urgent questions related especially to the Third World. Since our publisher wanted more secular language, we did not write explicitly of Christ. But what we there call life *is* Christ.

I have recently completed another book, co-authored this time with my dean, Joseph Hough. This book is on theological education.** One way to move the church toward global consciousness is to instill this in its professional leaders as they receive their formal education. That entails explicit presentation of major dimensions of global suffering and injustice and of the threat to the human future. But even more important, it entails practice in reflecting on particular issues confronting the church—in this case, primarily the white, North American, middle-class church—in view of the global context. This cuts against present tendencies to deal with local issues in their immediate context, while largely ignoring the writings that reflect on

---

* L. Charles Birch and John B. Cobb, Jr., *The Liberation of Life: From the Cell to the Community*. Cambridge University Press, 1981.

** Joseph C. Hough, Jr., and John B. Cobb, Jr., *Christian Identity and Theological Education*. Scholars Press, 1985.

global issues. There are still few good examples of reflecting as Christians on local issues in global context. We hope our book will model that type of thinking while it encourages embodying it in the core of seminary study.

A Christian Economic Theory

I have come to the conclusion that whatever scattered improvements there may be—in the situation of middle-class blacks or women in the United States, of workers in South Korea, of civil rights in Argentina or Brazil—the global situation will continue to decay as long as the present economic structures remain intact. I also am convinced that, with some obvious exceptions, these structures are consistent with dominant first-world economic theory. Although there is nothing about that theory that leads necessarily to some of the present abuses, overcoming those abuses would lessen the whole of human misery only a little. The theory itself must change for any major improvement to be possible.

Most of those who have come to this judgment—and they are many—have supposed that the alternative is socialism. This conclusion makes possible a commitment to an existing program undergirded by extensive theory. I, on the other hand, see little advantage in socialism. Its fundamental assumptions are as bound to Enlightenment modes of thought as are those of capitalism. Like capitalism, it is in tension with both the Bible and the ecological worldview.

I do feel some enthusiasm for current prospects in China. But I cannot overlook the enormous suffering and turmoil through which China has passed. That China did not succumb to still more destructive turmoil, that it came at last into the hands of more pragmatic, less ideological leadership, appears to be good fortune, or a result of peculiar features of the Chinese character—not an assured result of the theory. There is nothing in the ideology itself to prevent such experiments going the way of Campuchea.

The experiment with a mixed economy in Nicaragua appears the most promising of all the revolutions to date—if only the government of the United States will allow it to proceed. But it is the remarkable humanity of the leaders there, rather than their thinking about economics, that creates the hopeful situation. We cannot look to Nicaragua as a demonstration of the excellence of socialist theory.

Basically, my conviction is that the most important questions cut across the issues between capitalism and socialism. A central one is whether rapid industrialization of any sort is desirable. A second question is whether more is gained or lost by becoming a part of the system of international trade. Closely related to these is the priority given self-sufficiency in food. There is also the issue of land ownership. My answers to these questions differ from those of most capitalist and most socialist thinkers.

In *The Liberation of Life* (as well as in *Process Theology as Political Theology* *), I spelled out the overview of the global situation that underlies my approach to economic theory. I also listed a few of the very general principles derived therefrom. I am struggling to go beyond that.

Both of the books discussed in the preceding section depended on co-authorship with persons whose knowledge supplemented mine. To advance in economic thinking also will require collaboration.* * In any case, anything I can contribute to this vast area will be only one part of the fresh reflection that is beginning to emerge in many quarters. Perhaps a distinctive feature of my contribution will be the large role that the ecological perspective plays in my thinking.

Christian Repentance and Faith in Christ

Throughout the years, I have become more and more critical of Christianity and of the church I have known and loved. That is inevitable. To accept the critique of my own work as white, middle-class, North American, and male entails a criticism also of the community that shaped my interests and directed my attention. And there is more, much more, to be said in pointing out the mistakes, blindness, and sins of the dominant Christian community and its leadership.

At the same time that I have grown more critical, I also have become more sure of my identity as a Christian and as a churchman. It is our sins I confess, not those of others. It is clearer and clearer to me that to be a Christian and a churchman does not entail an exalted view of Christianity or of the church. But these reflections do press for an answer to the questions, What constitutes one's identity as Christian? What is the church?

I have spoken of Jesus, and also of Christ as the presence in the world of what was incarnate in Jesus. I understand the church as that community that lives by the memory of Jesus and commits itself to keep that memory alive and make it effective. It does so, normally, at

---

*John B. Cobb, Jr., *Process Theology as Political Theology*. Westminster Press, 1982.

** In 1989 I published with economist Herman Daly, *For the Common Good*. Beacon Press, 1989.

least, by reading the scriptures, preaching, and sacrament. Usually, this is supplemented by instruction, at least of catechumens.

Often the story is badly told, and the relevance for the present is distorted. Sometimes there is little effort to live by the implications drawn. Usually there is appalling blindness and complacency to much of what is important. Often those who are most sensitive to the real meaning of the gospel leave the church in disgust. The implications of the story are sometimes better expressed outside the church than in it. One could go on with such a litany of the frailty of the church. It does not have an admirable record. Nevertheless, this one thing it has done and does do. It keeps alive the memory of Israel's life with God as understood and appropriated through Jesus. This is of fundamental importance.

Christians are those whose identity is constituted by the memory that the church celebrates. In some measure, in changing times and places, they try to live by that memory. That directs them to Christ. Whereas Christ is effective everywhere, there is the potentiality, and often the actuality, of special effectiveness where Christ is named and consciously served. Alongside the sins of which we are called to repent, there also is much in our heritage for us to celebrate.

To be a Christian is not to suppose that Christians in general have served Christ well or that any of us are free from blindness and sin. It is instead to trust in the Christ who judges, forgives, and heals, through creation and transformation, not in the church alone, but throughout the world. By trusting Christ, I am free to confess my own sins and those of my community, however appalling have been their scope and their consequences.

There is, then, no essence, kernel, or core of Christianity as those are usually understood. There is no doctrine the absence of which would demonstrate that one is not a Christian. There is no essential pattern of behavior. The effort to fix the meaning of "Christian" in these ways is an expression not of faith, but of a lack of faith. As H. Richard Niebuhr taught us,* what Christians have in common is a center to the memory out of which they live. That center is the story of Jesus and the apostolic witness to him. To whatever extent one attains identity around that center, one is a Christian.

There is a matter of degree involved. Since the Enlightenment, the lives even of Christians have been so fragmented that different

---

* H. Richard Niebuhr, *The Meaning of Revelation.* Macmillan, 1941.

portions may be only slightly related to one another. A Christian scholar or scientist may operate much of the time in terms of a discipline and its norms, hardly connecting them with a personal life for which Jesus is the center. Much greater fragmentation is possible. One way of considering the process of Christian growth is to see how Jesus can become the center of more and more of life, thus overcoming its fragmentation.

Global Theology Beyond Disciplines

I have spoken of theology as thinking self-consciously as a Christian. The fact that one both thinks and is a Christian does not guarantee that one will think *as* a Christian. The Enlightenment has taught us to compartmentalize our thinking. Also, one may think *as* a Christian without doing so self-consciously. Thinking as a Christian means that the thinking is correlated with that part of one's world that is centered in Jesus. Such thinking is inevitably affected by the meanings and values that are present in that world. But if such connections are not self-conscious, they will not be critically examined with respect to their appropriateness to the center.

There is nothing inherently superior about self-conscious thinking. Self-consciousness can be inhibiting. But it does have certain advantages. What is thought self-consciously can be explained to others. The connections made can be examined, and when that examination reveals errors, they can be corrected. It is this self-conscious kind of Christian thinking about important questions that I call theology.

In this sense, reflecting about economic questions in global context self-consciously as a Christian *is* theology. It does not, of course, fall within the academic *discipline* of theology. Indeed, it does not fall within any of the Enlightenment disciplines at all. My own theology leads me to hope for the end of the discipline of theology and of all the disciplines, not so that thinking will become less disciplined, less self-critical, or less honest, but so that it may participate in serving the real needs of the world. Christ calls us to disciplined thought beyond all the disciplines.

Part
II

A
Thinking
Church

4

Can the Church Think Again?

There was a time when the church thought. The church out-thought its competitors in the Roman Empire. The church became in that period the cutting edge of thought, and once it won its battle against pagan philosophy—which included incorporating much of that philosophy within itself—it became for a thousand years the one bearer of thought in Christian Europe. The period climaxed in the thirteenth and fourteenth centuries in one of the world's great ages of intellectual vitality.

This intellectual vitality spilled over into topics on the periphery of the traditional interests of the church. The church allowed and even encouraged this broadening of interests that we call, somewhat misleadingly, the Renaissance. Most of the new thinking was done by churchmen, lay and clerical, and it reflected much more deeply than was then recognized—or is even acknowledged today—the achievements of the church's thinking. But what emerged was no longer the thinking of the church. In retrospect, we may see that the Renaissance, the Enlightenment, and the Romantic Movement were Christian, but they were autonomous in relation to the church and often experienced as threats to it.

An Occasional Paper issued by the United Methodist Board of Higher Education and Ministry in 1976.

The church did not stop thinking when autonomous thinking emerged. The Reformation was, among other things, the thinking of the church informed by and responding to Renaissance humanism. As late as the seventeenth century, the issues that tore the church grasped many, even most, of the best minds of Christendom. But looking back from the twentieth century, we no longer notice this, because the thinking that bore fruit was not of the church.

By the eighteenth century, the church's thinking had become defensive. Creative, mind-transforming energies of thought were outside the church. There were still many intelligent, learned, and dedicated churchmen, but they did not devote themselves to advancing the frontiers of thought. Instead, their task was to adapt Christian belief to a changing situation and to justify its continuation in this new form. In the process, men such as Bishop Berkeley in England and Jonathan Edwards in America engaged in profound intellectual analysis at the frontier of the thinking of their day. Thus, some of the church's thought became a part of our general intellectual history rather than only a part of the church's adaptation and defense. But, as a part of that history, it was built upon not by churchmen, but by an autonomous philosophy.

At the beginning of the nineteenth century in Germany, there was another of those rare great periods of intellectual ferment, and it brought the thinking of the church into closer relationship to the frontier of thought than it had been since the Reformation. The Enlightenment had run its course, and its intellectual superficiality had become apparent. Its strength had been its iconoclasm, and if its achievements were to survive, they must be rooted in much deeper principles. When thought probes deeply, it inevitably enters the sphere of basic questions where Christian faith has meaning and relevance. Hence, the Christian faith became thematically important for this great period, in the world of such giants as Kant, Hegel, and Schleiermacher. All were fundamentally post-Enlightenment Christians, and Schleiermacher was a leading churchman.

This remarkable event gave to the church its one great chance in the modern world to share again in the carrying forward of thought. To some extent, in the German world, it responded. In the German universities, where the best thinking of the West occurred, Protestant theology held its head high, attracted its share of the finest thinkers, and played a significant cultural and intellectual role. Through its theological faculties, the church continued to think. The debt of the whole of Christendom to their achievement is not yet fully appreciated.

Nevertheless, the promise of new beginnings was not fully realized. Outside the German Protestant world, the church continued its defensive style, and even in Germany the relation of the church to its thinkers was an uneasy one. The theologians were torn between the basic conservatism in the churches and the radical results of their own thinking insofar as this genuinely participated in shaping the frontier of thought. Some, such as David Friedrich Strauss, followed their thinking outside the church. Others learned the art of moderation and sophisticated compromise, thereby precluding the possibility of genuine participation in the thinking of the West.

Ernst Troeltsch was the last great expression in the church's participation in this thinking of German idealism. He sought passionately to understand and affirm the Christian claim to universal finality through probing Christian history to the depths in the context of the new global history of religions. But his results did not support him, and he reluctantly surrendered his role as theologian to accept a chair of philosophy.

After World War I, the church's thinkers adopted a quite different strategy. Just as the thought of the Enlightenment was bankrupt by the end of the eighteenth century, so German idealism appeared bankrupt by the end of the First World War. Whereas Kant, Hegel, and Schleiermacher had saved the achievements of the Enlightenment by subsuming them into a deeper and more Christian matrix, Barth, Brunner, and Gogarten opposed to the emptiness of secular thought and culture the transcendent Word of God. The church's thinkers dared to place the church's faith over against modern thought and the faith of the church itself as the cutting edge of Western thought.

It was a bold attempt, and it won many important battles. But it was doomed to failure. The pluralistic achievements of the modern world are far too great, and far too important for the Western spirit, to be relegated to secondary status before the church's proclamation of the Word of God. The actual effect was to ghettoize the church's thinking in Germany as it had long since been ghettoized in the rest of Christendom. The church withdrew from its sharing in the ongoing thought of the West in the one place where, since the Reformation, it had continued to share effectively—namely, in Protestant Germany. Now its relative role in the German university is reduced, and the continuation of Christian theology as a discipline within the German university is under attack. There are pressures to transform it officially, as in Sweden, into the objective study of religious phenomena. Meanwhile, much of what goes on in theological faculties is already of this sort.

In America, during the great days of German theology, the church thought very little. The best scholars studied in Germany and brought home to America modified versions of what they had learned. These provided some intellectual respectability to the church. More important were American movements in philosophy, often motivated by religious interests, which reduced the gap between thinking and church life. William James, Josiah Royce, and for Methodists, Borden Parker Bowne, made it possible for American Protestants in the early twentieth century to enter the world of thought without abandoning their faith. They offered the American church at the beginning of this century a possibility analogous to that offered the German church at the beginning of the nineteenth century. The major sustained attempt to make use of this opportunity was by American Baptists in the Divinity School that became the nucleus of the University of Chicago. There the church thought in intimate connection with dominant currents of thinking in the university as a whole. The experiment survived into the fifties. But by then, it was so cut off from the church that it could no longer count as the church's thinking.

The great period of denominational theological education in America began after World War II, and it still continues. Though the American church lacked organs of thought, it recognized the importance of education for ministers. Further, for the most part, it believed in intellectual freedom and was willing for its seminaries to participate in the world of the university. As if to prepare for the decline of the great tradition of German theology, Americans created, or radically strengthened, scores of potential centers through which the church might learn to think again.

Despite the availability of well-supported institutions, immediate prospects are not promising. We live in the aftermath of the collapse of the neoorthodox superstructure of church theology that occurred in the sixties. Church theology was bound up with that form and has not yet found a new one. The pressure for university acceptance drives toward specialized expertise and discourages the church's thinking.

But the real problem is not to be viewed in this narrow way. It is a fundamental historical-systematic question. Can the church think today? I hope that my brief survey of the history helps to explain what I mean by that question. I do not mean to ask trivially whether committed Christians can think seriously and well about something or other. Of course, there are committed Christians in all fields of learning, and some make thoughtful contributions. And, of course, committed Christians can and do engage in critical study of our own tradition, using and refining the latest scholarly methods. Further, there are committed Christians who sincerely and unabashedly propound the Christian faith as if the past three centuries had not occurred.

The question is whether the church can understand its faith in a way that enters into the current state of the cultural and intellectual life of the West. Can it, sustained by its faith, enter into and advance the frontiers of Western thinking? To these questions the answer that has sounded more and more often among the theologically educated in the past ten years is "No! If we are to think, we must separate ourselves from the church. The tradition and images of the church combined with its actual present character are an impediment to thinking." Among those who answer in this way, some, such as Thomas Altizer, are radical Christians for whom the church is an anachronistic form, and others, such as Sam Keen, have rejected Christianity altogether.

I wish that I could tell you that we professors of theology in United States seminaries have a clear and confident answer to these "no-sayers." But collectively we have no answer at all. Of course, as individuals, we have ideas and proposals, but we are fragmented and confused. The proposals of one professor rarely commend themselves to others. There is no center by which we all take our bearings. The church today is not thinking.

Consider again the problem. The concrete life of the church largely reflects the society and culture of which it is a part. Traditional images and doctrines are retained and used for limited purposes. These images and doctrines seem to belong to a world that is remote from both the popular culture expressed in most of the church's life and the cutting edge of creative thought. What, then, would it mean for such a church to think?

Probably what the church wants, unconsciously, is for theologians to explain the inherited images and doctrines in ways that support current church life, while assuring people of the importance of activities that have come to seem trivial. To some extent, that can be done and is being done. It may be a good thing to do. But whether it is worth doing depends on the results of another and more authentic form of thinking, which faces the question of importance and human meaning in the context of the deepest understanding of our human situation now available. Can the church engage in *that* form of thinking? If not, is it to learn the norms by which to measure itself from the psychological and social sciences? There is no doubt that most of the church's actual self-evaluation today is based on such autonomous norms, but insofar as this procedure is accepted as standard—insofar, that is, as the church ceases to generate any norms of its own—has the church not ceased to be the church? The question of whether the church can think again is hardly separable from the question of whether the church can endure as church.

Whether the church can endure as church is a question that is different from the question of whether our denominational institutions and congregations can survive. In this country, we can easily imagine that more and more of our congregations can evolve into voluntary organizations that provide desired services to their members and in their communities. These services can be psychological, educational, cultural, recreational, and even religious. The offering of them can be motivated by Christian concern for the whole person. But the specific activities designed to produce such motivation might cease, or at least become optional. This scenario is worked out enthusiastically in Ernest Harrison's book *Church Without God*, and many congregations have drifted toward such a model without full consciousness of what they are doing. Even retaining Sunday morning preaching and worship as the central congregational activity—as Harrison does not—would not insure that the substantive change is avoided.

We could hope that the church's schools of theology would stand against this drift. Here the tradition is taught—and taught well, I might add. And courses in theology are often lively and enlightening, even if for the most part they only rehash the church's thinking in earlier generations. But biblical scholars, church historians, and systematic theologians do not explain the meaning of the ideas they present for the actual life of the church. That, we think, is for students to work out, aided by the faculty that teaches the arts of ministry. But what occurs there? What can occur? Can professors of pastoral counseling do more with the writings of theologians than make occasional references to them? It seems not. Must they not take their norms from personality theory hewed out in relation to clinical data? Should they not follow the cutting edge of that discipline? And are not the church's thinkers absent from that cutting edge?

If the answers to these questions are affirmative, professors of pastoral counseling do well to turn away from the church's thinkers for the norms of their discipline. But what, then, makes pastoral counseling pastoral? The fact that it is done by pastors? But what makes pastors Christian? Their leadership of churches? But what makes churches Christian? Lingering habits, perhaps?

The last stronghold for theology in the church's life has been the proclamation of the Word. As long as ministers know what the church's thinkers teach, they have the option of declaring that message, even if they cannot relate it to the rest of the life of the church. But when the church ceases to think, even those preachers who would like to preach the church's gospel are driven to look elsewhere for their messages.

It would be comforting to think that the collapse of theology means the return to basics or to the Bible. It is true that it does practically mean at times a return to simplistic forms of evangelicalism or fundamentalism. The church can stop caring whether its message is effectively related to the cutting edge of thought and deal with simple people in cultural ghettos. This has its advantages, but the resultant practices and attitudes are distasteful to the sensitive and crumble when exposed to the dominant culture. It is a temporary and desperate expedient.

There are others who see little importance in the internal life of the church. They are concerned that the church's energies be mobilized for social reform or the liberation of the oppressed. Among the liberation theologians, some *are* sharing in the cutting edge of thought today insofar as that thought is the ideology of repressed groups seeking freedom. If the basic condition of the church were healthier, their leadership might become significant. But we can hardly expect to mobilize for sacrificial action in the world a community that does not experience its inherited faith as relevant to its own internal activities. And we can hardly expect persons outside the church to be moved by a prophetic word that cannot be heard within it.

Let me put the problem another way. Christian faith is bound up with loving God holistically. One may be a good Republican, a good mechanic, a good husband, a good soccer player, and a good practitioner of transcendental meditation, all at once, with no particular relevance of one involvement to the others except as they compete for time. But if a person is truly Christian, every dimension of life is involved. Christ must be all in all.

What does this mean for a pluralistic society in which the church does not think? For some of the most devout, it means withdrawal from the world into a small sphere from which activities not centered in Christ are shut out. One reads only what is Christ-centered and associates on an equal basis only with other Christ-centered people. Since the actual decisions about the course of history are made on other grounds and on the basis of a situation that is not Christ-centered, one cuts oneself off from all that. Something like this characterized the early church and reappeared in vital sectarian movements. In the early church, however, it was the matrix in which a new spirit was nurtured around insights and sensibilities that probed beyond and beneath the general culture, whereas today the sectarian groups can survive only by ignoring what is available to be known and felt elsewhere. Sectarian science and history, for example, are markedly inferior to science and history as practiced in the secular sphere.

Others seeking holistic faith practice it in the pluralistic world. They take their science from scientists and their history from historians. They allow the objective sphere to operate on its own terms. For Christ to be all in all means for them that a Christlike spirit can pervade whatever activities they engage in. Pietists thus seek to be holistically Christian inwardly, while filling in society whatever role falls their lot.

The feature of pietism that has called forth the most extensive critique thus far is its failure to recognize that the structures of society are unchristian. If one tries to be Christlike within such structure, one may in fact help them to survive, when what is needed is their replacement by more just and liberating structures.

This familiar critique is sound as far as it goes, and it has led to some valuable consequences. Denominational leadership has taken stands for human rights and for moves toward more equitable distribution of power and wealth. But no vision of a Christian society has emerged. Instead, Christians at their best debate the merits of economic and political theories generated without conscious regard for Christian faith. Most allow their normal prejudices to govern their actions. Only occasionally do issues arise that elicit substantial reformist response from the churches, and these responses mirror the responses of people of goodwill in the society as a whole. Limited groups within the church are able to merge their Christian conviction with the ideologies of oppressed people, but they lack the leverage to move other equally committed Christians.

The point there is not to criticize sectarians, pietists, or liberationists. The point is, instead, that in a church that does not think, nothing better is possible. Christ cannot be all in all for believers unless they can see that science and history, art and politics, economic and social institutions, as well as personal morality and private spirituality, can all serve him and be taken up into him. But that is in no way evident today when a fragmented church faces a fragmented world and borrows fragmented bits of wisdom without any principle of selection.

I am not simply discussing the problem of my professional discipline. I am also reflecting on the status and future of ministry.

What does it mean to minister in a church that does not think? Can it mean anything other than the adaptation of an existing institution to programs that meet the felt needs of some group in the community in which it is located? Is there any reason to suppose that the result of this procedure will be a Christian church? How can a church that does not think answer such questions?

We have already become so accustomed to getting along without thinking that it may be too late. More markedly than ten years ago, ministers know that their *actual* role is the priestly one of visiting and counseling, marrying and burying, and being present in crises. To the performance of this role, the study of the Christian tradition appears irrelevant. Ministers are no longer looked to as teachers or spiritual guides, and the prophetic element is not desired in the pulpit. Hence, the continuing education for which they truly feel a need is predominantly refresher courses in the arts of ministry.

This role definition also affects young people entering seminary. They no longer view the ministry as a learned profession. The task is not the mediation of the gospel or the tradition to a community of the faithful; it is dealing with the hurts of people and helping them to grow through fellowship. If Bible study and theology can help to prepare one to fulfill this ministry, fine. But if not, they are perceived as the academic requirements of a faculty that is insensitive to the reality of parish life.

The institutional church that supports the seminary measures it primarily by the number of effective ministers it produces. The study of the tradition in more than superficial ways makes little direct contribution to success. Indeed, if it produces a tension between the young minister's understanding of the norms of the gospel and the felt needs of the people, the study of the tradition proves counterproductive. Sensing this, many of those who become serious about the faith decide for teaching rather than parish ministry.

Thus far, I have tried to picture as accurately as I can the history and present state of the church's thinking and the results of its collapse for the life of the church. The picture is bleak, but it has its bright side. The church continues to support institutions for thinking even when the major demands upon these institutions move them in other directions. There is widespread recognition of the weakness of the present situation along with a ferment of confused ideas. These may be the death-throes of theology, but they also may be the birth-pangs of a new period in which the church will think again. If so, it will be chiefly because the autonomous development of thought brings about a situation to which the church's contribution will have evident relevance. I believe that this development is in full course.

When the basic principles by which a society lives are felt as secure and evident, theology is largely irrelevant. The Christian tradition may support some of the principles and oppose others, but the support is not needed and the opposition makes no difference. When the basic principles by which a society lives are uncertain and confused, however, then a critical perspective, brought to bear upon them from a long and honorable tradition by people who live from it, has its apparent importance.

In the sixties, we entered a period of radical uncertainty. The basic structures of relationships between the sexes have become problematic through the sexual revolution and the feminist movement, combined with the decline of permanent monogamous marriage and the nuclear family. The ideology of the sexual revolution and women's liberation raises the most basic questions about the meaning of human equality and its relation to organic social forms, as well as about the relation of bodily enjoyment and work to human fulfillment. The meaning and value of sacrificial service have become questionable. Love is a word that now appears usually in quotes.

The ecological movement challenged our assumptions in equally fundamental ways. It showed us that our cherished ideas of the infinite value of human life or the sacredness of human personality are not self-evident goods but rather have spawned developments that threaten the possibilities for a decent life for our children. It made us aware that our sense of transcendence over nature is both exaggerated and dangerous. It renewed a lost sense of limits with respect to human aspirations. It forced us to reappraise our refusal to consider humanity as a biological species. It has challenged our almost unconscious assumptions that there is a technological solution to all our problems.

The ecological movement combined with a new awareness of the limits of natural resources and the decline of many of our social institutions has raised questions about our fundamental conviction that our basic human problems can be dealt with best by economic growth. The desirability of the increase of the gross national product is now questionable. We are looking at the goods that we have prized afresh, and we are reconsidering whether they are the most important ones. In this context, we are questioning in a new way the value of free compulsory education and our system of medical care. Indeed, the whole structure of Western industrial humanistic culture is exposed as problematic.

Perhaps it is for this reason that the wisdom of the Orient and of primitive peoples is no longer perceived as quaint. We are at last ready to recognize that the West is one of the many civilizations the world has seen, with its merits and limitations like all the rest. World history is no longer Western history, expanding to include other countries as these are discovered by Western explorers, but is in truly a plurality of partly independent histories that are now at last weaving together into global history.

In this ferment of fundamental change, the church has a golden opportunity to share in new processes of thought. Theological issues are raised on all sides. Yet, the church is strangely silent. It seems not to know how to participate in the new currents of thought. I believe this is because past patterns of the church's thinking do not work today.

How can the church think responsibly? There have been two main types of answers to this question. I will call them legalist and essentialist, and I will explain how I see them.

The legalist approach seeks specific teachings in the tradition that can be brought to bear on current issues. For example, on the questions raised by the sexual revolution and women's liberation, one seeks in the Bible, or in the received teachings of the church, relevant and authoritative answers. At one extreme, this can be biblical prooftexting, where any teaching found anywhere in the Bible can be cited with little or no regard for its context or its relation to differing teachings found elsewhere in the sacred writings. Or, the latest pronouncement of an ecclesiastical body can be taken as the final and definitive word. But the legalist approach can be much subtler and more sophisticated than this. It can recognize the historical development of the teaching and identify the climactic expression in Jesus or perhaps in Paul as authoritative. Until recently, many laws on marriage and divorce in both church and state were based on the authority of Matthew 19:9. But legalist thinking can take historical development still more seriously and deny final authority to any biblical text, seeking instead the principle or germinal idea that gains expression in different ways in different contexts. For example, one might decide that the goodness of human sexuality as a divine gift is the principle underlying the historical development of biblical teaching and that it is this principle we should apply afresh today in our new situation. Clearly this is much less "legalist" than is prooftexting, but it represents the same effort to identify a fixed authoritative norm from which all Christian teaching in the area of sex is to be derived.

The essentialists carry the movement from prooftext to principle a step further. They deny that Christian faith is bound up with an unchanging set of principles underlying its teaching about the several areas of human life. They recognize that a Christian ethics of unchanging principles is a sophisticated form of legalism. They seek instead to grasp the essence of Christianity as such. This may be seen as trust in the redemptive efficacy of Christ's death, or the infinite value of human personality, or commitment to the way of love, or the assurance of final fulfillment. It may be a state of being or a mode of existence, such as authentic existence or the new being.

The essentialist calls on the church to address itself to each issue freshly from its own essence. The church should be free from commitment to its own past teachings or even to specific teachings of Jesus or Paul. Indeed, explicit past teachings may need to be reversed in faithfulness to the Christian essence.

However, neither legalists nor essentialists are able today to lead the church into thinking again. Both bring *to* the present situation something fixed and settled in the distant past. Insofar as this something has definiteness and specificity, it comes as alien to the actuality of the present situation. It appears to impede that discussion rather than further it. Insofar as this something is indefinite, it seems simply irrelevant to the present discussion. It functions to liberate the Christian to participate in the discussion without inhibition, but it contributes nothing Christian to it. In neither of these types of theology does the church think.

There is irony here, for in the formulation of the principles and of the essence, real thinking often occurs. This is apparent in the history of such principles and essences. Those who most strongly proclaim their formulations as capturing what has been and must always be Christian usually arrive at their conclusions by interaction with the sources through sensibilities that have been sharpened in the current situation. They see and appraise the sources in a fresh light, and no sooner than their contribution is made public, others work to refine and transcend it. This history of principles and essences reveals the church as thinking in a way that its application to the problems of the day does not.

If this is so, then theologians should cease to deceive themselves. The church's "essence" today is different from its "essence" yesterday, and the effort to fasten it onto tomorrow must fail if the church lives at all. Christian history is not a process of expressing an unchanging essence in changing circumstances. Neither is it a progressive unfolding of an original, unchanging essence. The church is a living movement that maintains its identity through the memory of its history—not by preserving an unchanging essence.

The history the church remembers is not static. It changes in at least three ways. First, and most obviously, every passing year adds a new chapter, or a least a new paragraph. Second, it is continuously changed and expanded by the work of historians. Third—most importantly, but still most controversially—it grows by the engrafting into it of histories that were previously foreign to it. Thus in the West, the church came to live by the memory of Greek philosophy and Roman law as well as by the memory of Jesus and the prophets. The church can indigenize itself in Asia and Africa only as, in similar ways, it expands its memory to include their histories. And the church can fulfill its mission of universality only as its memory extends to include global history.

If this is the right way to think of the church, then for the church to think cannot be to bring to bear upon the present something that is alien to that present. The church thinks in the present. The present stirs its memories. What was half-forgotton becomes vivid and important. What was obscure becomes luminous. What was rejected as alien becomes central. The new pattern of memory created by the immersion of the church in the present in turn illumines the present, and the church can share what it sees there with others. In the process, the church itself is changed as it expresses its new pattern of memory and understanding in its own life.

This does not mean that the church will have its own teaching on each subject to set over against everyone else's ideas. Far from it. The church will remember how much it has learned from others in the past and be open to being taught again. But it will be open as its own memories open it, and it will learn by integrating new memories with old. It will not abandon its own memories as a basis of its normative judgments.

What I am describing is the liberation of the church and its thinking. The conditions, especially in our own country, are ripe. Indeed, in principle this liberation is part of "the liberty wherewith Christ has made us free" (Gal. 5:1). And our own country's history of pluralism has already made real the liberation of the church and its thinking to a large extent. Yet, this freedom is exercised haltingly and with anxiety that its expression may somehow be faithless to the liberator. If in this third century of liberty in the United States the American church grasps confidently its own liberty to think and live, it can lead toward a healthy global Christianity. If not, we will continue to lose the finest of our daughters and sons. For if not, the church must fundamentally be understood to be what it has been, and for the most sensitive and perceptive of our children, what it has been is not good enough for now. This has been brought home to me repeatedly in recent months in three recent encounters.

The first is with one of the most brilliant of today's feminists, one who sought her place in the church, experienced rejection, and has become one of its most bitter and effective critics. We might dismiss this as a practical problem of church organization and discipline, reflecting extra-Christian social practices, but that is superficial. She has shown that male dominance of the institution is bound up with the maleness of deity and the male perspective dominating all the church's thinking in the past. If the church is what the church has been, then the church *is* sexist to the core. She as a feminist must oppose it.

A second encounter was with a leading male theologian who gave up seminary teaching some years ago. I had thought that intellectual doubts about the truth of the church's teaching were at the heart of his unwillingness to continue to identify himself as a Christian theologian. But no, he said, for him the central problem is Christianity's anti-Semitism. After Auschwitz, he held, one cannot be a Christian, for one sees to what end the church's essential teaching leads. If, for the church to be the church, it must proclaim, as it proclaimed, that the one savior of all is the one whom the Jews rejected and continue to reject, then to be a Christian is to be anti-Semitic.

A third encounter was with an able young professor of religion in a state college. He had ceased to be a Christian, he said, because to be a Christian was to reject the truth and value that he was discovering in Oriental thought. He could appreciate the truth and value that he was discovering in Oriental thought. He could appreciate the truth and value in Christianity, but his integrity required that he be equally open to other traditions. If the church is what it always has been, namely a community that proclaims its message in such a way as to disparage the messages of alternative faith communities, then he does right to separate himself from the church.

These are people the church needs if it is to think again. Much of what they are saying must be appropriated by the church even though it is being spoken against the church. This can and will happen in time, even though those who speak have left forever. But how much better if those children of the church who attack it for what it has been could recognize themselves as faithful in that attack to the life of the church that is the spirit of Christ! How much better for the church, which could then so much more easily appropriate their truth! And how much better for them, who could then draw upon the expanding and changing memories of the church as well as share in their reshaping and extension!

If the church in its thinking recognizes what has always been the case, that it is a living historical movement most vital when it changes in creative response to its situation, then it can hold and support its children in their prophetic work. And in and through them, the church can think again.

5

Christian Universality Revisited

In the current scene, the division within Christianity grows wider. On the one side are those who have paid sensitive attention to criticisms coming from many quarters. This group has come to see that in many ways Christianity has been arrogant and oppressive. Members of this group are determined not to continue to make the affirmations and claims that have had these destructive consequences. As a result, this group is characterized more by its hesitations and negations than by clear positive affirmations of its faith. On the other side are those firmly committed to Christianity as they have known it, usually in conservative garb. For the most part, they continue to say and do the things that have oppressed others in the past. They continue to make strong claims for Christian universality and to act upon them.

My sympathies are with the former group. I am convinced that faithfulness to Christ requires us to hear about our sins and to repent of them. This is just as true when the sins are collective ones committed in the name of Christ as when they are personal violations of ethical rules. Indeed, there is something particularly distressing

---

An address delivered at De Pauw University, Greencastle, Indiana, in October 1989.

about sins self-righteously committed in the name of Christ. We can forgive ourselves for our failure to live up to the high standard of conduct we associate with Christ. But when in the name of Christ we persecute Jesus' own people and oppress women, then we blaspheme the most precious name we have, the name before whom we hope that some day every knee will bow. If we must choose between a luke-warm Christianity that has ceased to do massive evil in the name of Christ, on the one hand, and a self-confident Christianity that continues to be oppressive on the other, we should certainly choose the former. But surely we can do better!

Frankly, I have little hope for the future of a church that knows only what it does not believe, and then concentrates upon its institutional life. It cannot expect its own children to take it seriously. It cannot win new followers. It can only wither and die. Nothing can be more urgent for the church's theologians than the positive reformulation of the church's teaching in such a way that wholehearted belief can become a truly positive factor in personal and public life.

There are several horizons within which the work of reformulation should be carried on. Today, I will talk about the horizon of world religions. There can be no question but that Christians have sinned against other religious traditions and their members in the name of Christ. This has been especially marked in relation to the Jews. But primal peoples have also suffered massively at our hands, and there is hardly a non-Christian religious tradition that cannot tell some story of Christian oppression.

Most of this is rooted in our universal claims about Christ. If Christ is the one savior of all the world, we have thought, then our task is to displace all those communities that do not acknowledge this. With so much at stake, hardly any tactic has seemed to Christians too harsh to use. We have justified crusades, pogroms, imperialism, colonialism, and even slavery as instruments of Christian expansion.

Alongside this arrogant imposition of our will on others, there has been serious reflection about how Christianity is in fact related to the other religious communities and traditions. In the past two centuries, many of the church's greatest thinkers have taken the global religious scene as the context for constructing their theologies. In each of the three main responses to which I want to direct your attention, the initial formulations retained strong universal affirmation. In all three cases, the course of thought has led to dropping the universal claims. The reasons for this change have been admirable, but the total effect on the church is troubling. My effort in this lecture will be to suggest a way in which the church can recover the note of universality in its affirmations without renewing the arrogance that has caused so much harm. But first, I want to summarize the three modern traditions that have undertaken to understand Christianity in the context of religious pluralism.

II

Pride of place in modern Protestant theology belongs to Friedrich Schleiermacher. He was the first theologian to order his whole theological program in the context of his understanding of global religion. He depicted Christianity as one religion among others. In this sense, he inaugurated the move toward relativizing Christian faith. But Schleiermacher explained the nature of religion and the forms it could take so as to present the monotheistic faiths as clearly superior, and among the monotheistic faiths he made Christianity appear to the be the best. In his hands, the description of diversity became an argument for superiority. His readers were not led to question their wholehearted commitment to Christ.

Schleiermacher's achievement was a brilliant one, convincing to many. But once Christianity was understood as a religion and was viewed in its relation to other religions, it became important to check his definition of religion and his characterization of the others. His definition of religion as the feeling of absolute dependence did not hold up well under this examination. Other, more plausible, candidates appeared. Early in this century, Rudolf Otto, with more empirical information than had been available to Schleiermacher, concluded that the distinctively religious quality in experience is the sense of the holy. With this judgment, he was able to carry out a program similar to Schleiermacher's. He, too, portrayed Christianity as the highest form of religion.

The last great example of this style of theology was Paul Tillich. For him, what distinguishes religion is ultimate concern. This ultimate concern is truly directed to Being Itself, and on this we are wholly dependent for our existence; so he could capture the truth in Schleiermacher's insight. Also, he believed that the sense of the holy is directly related to our ultimate concern; so Otto, too, was vindicated. And Tillich, like Schleiermacher and Otto, was able to describe the situation in such a way as to present Christianity as the fullness of religion. But in his last years, Tillich had second thoughts. His personal experience with Buddhists in Japan and extensive working with Mircea Eliade led him to see that the situation is more complex than he had realized. He called for a theological approach that took the data of the history of religions more seriously and did not insist on Christian superiority.

Since Tillich, the quest to understand Christianity as a religion has continued, but its leaders have increasingly assumed a rough parity among the great living faiths. The question is now not one of ranking them so as to display Christian superiority, but viewing them as parallel ways of embodying the common religious essence. This effort is often carried on in dialogue with representatives of the other traditions, so the tendency to view all from one perspective is checked. Each is allowed to define itself.

Approaching matters in this way has made it very difficult to discover a common element in all religious experience. There continue to be efforts. But now the commonality is sometimes sought in the religious object instead. Realizing that "God" cannot be acceptable to all traditions as the object of religious concerns, other terms are tried, such as "the ultimate," or "the Real." All the religions are then viewed as diverse ways of orienting life to this common reality.

When this approach is adopted, much of what is important to Christians appears quite relative. Not only is Christ seen as one among many ways that people have come to understand the religious object and to orient themselves to it, the same is true of a personal God, and even of anything that can be called "God" at all. This does not mean that we Christians should cease acknowledging the importance of Jesus to us, or stop imaging the religious object as a personal deity. But if we follow this line of reasoning, then we know, even as we do this, that Jesus' importance is only for us, and that the God we worship is only one possible image or symbol for the religious object. Most of what we care about must be recognized now as belonging to our images of this object and not to the object as such. Clearly, no universal claims for Christian faith are involved.

The second great theological tradition that placed Christianity clearly in the global context was initiated by Hegel. Whereas Schleiermacher focused on religious experience, Hegel reflected on the place of Christianity in the unfolding drama of the human spirit or *Geist*. For Hegel, *Geist* had a history, and that meant a linear chronological development. This is the history of civilization understood in terms of basic modes of human self-understanding. Its progress is identified with the emergence and growth of personal freedom and of the institutions that embody it. In Hegel's vision, the beginning of this development of Spirit was in China, the culmination in Christian Europe. Again, but in a different way than for Schleiermacher, Christianity is the final answer.

During the nineteenth century, historical knowledge about other parts of the world increased greatly. The Hegelian story needed to be retold. The task was taken up by a man richly qualified as a scholar and a thinker: Ernst Troeltsch. He, too, thought that he could show Christianity as the culmination, this time because of its peculiar ability to transcend human cultures. But as Troeltsch pursued his research, he made two discoveries. First, Christianity was more culture-bound than he had supposed. Second, certain other religions, such as those of India, were more able to transcend cultural boundaries than he had thought. Troeltsch retained a distinction between the higher religions and the merely tribal ones, seeing the former as able to displace the latter. But he finally acknowledged that, among the higher religions, each was best in the cultural sphere in which it flourished. There was no neutral standpoint from which one could be declared superior to the others.

Since Troeltsch, the great majority of the study of the history of religions has separated itself from theological questions. For this new discipline, the task is simply to understand more accurately, without making judgments of value or truth. This academic discipline has flourished. So far as it has theological implications, these are that we should acknowledge that each community has its own forms of life and thought, that each has its own norms and values, that ours are no better and no worse than others. The relativization of Christianity is complete.

The third response to religious pluralism can be called confessional. Karl Barth saw clearly and profoundly the consequences of locating Christianity in the wider context of religion in general or of cultural history. Doing so directed attention away from the content of the Christian faith itself. That faith was in the saving work of God in Jesus Christ. Neither Christian religious experience nor the role of Christianity in universal history can take the place of what God has done and will do. The role of Christians is to witness to God's work rather than to talk about the superiority of our religious experience or our great historical achievements. In this way, we can at once be faithful to our scriptures and avoid arrogance.

Barth undertook not only to undercut Christian arrogance but also to soften the excessive concern of Christians with proselytizing. He emphasized that the right witness to what God has done in Jesus Christ is to assure all people that they are already saved in Christ. They are saved whether or not they believe. Of course, many of the advantages of being saved are not obtained until one believes; for unless one believes, one will still engage anxiously in the futile quest for salvation. Hence, there are reasons for sharing the message. But the motive is not to save souls from hell, a motive that has led to many abuses. Further, in general, members of Christian churches and those outside are pictured in much the same fashion. We are all trying to save ourselves by works rather accepting the salvation that has already been accomplished for us.

Despite Barth's sensitivity to the implications of the Christian gospel for outsiders and his brilliant formulations, few who have been deeply involved with persons from other traditions are satisfied. As individual human beings, these persons are neither disparaged nor excluded from salvation. But as believers in other traditions, they are told that all they hold most dear is worthless and irrelevant. They cannot recognize themselves in Barth's account of the anxious efforts at self-salvation. They are offended that once again Christianity alone is depicted as knowing the way of salvation.

Barth's influence continues today, but generally in very moderated form. Negatively, there are many who reject the effort to locate Christianity, as if from without, in the horizon of religion or world history. Positively, they agree that the task of the Christian theologian is to witness faithfully to the biblical message. But now that message is not understood as making supernatural or cosmic affirmations about God's activity in Jesus Christ. It is understood as fashioning an imagistic home in which believers can live.

A number of theologians of Barthian background have adopted, from anthropologist Richard Geertz, the idea of a cultural-linguistic system, and have applied this to Christianity. In their view, the church should be the place where people learn that system and how to operate with it. The problem today is that the language of the church has become merged with that of a secular culture. Christian faith is thereby threatened. We need to intensify the inner life of our congregations by incorporating the people into the cultural-linguistic system that is Christianity.

It should be clear that just as the other moves of which I spoke among the heirs of Schleiermacher and Hegel radically relativized Christianity, this one did so as well. That is, all three give up the effort to show that Christianity is superior to other religions and acknowledge that it is simply one among many. Still, there is a profound difference between this third, confessional, stance and the others, especially among the heirs of Schleiermacher. Whereas that development tends to reduce emphasis on what is distinctive of Christianity in favor of the common element it shares with all, this one takes the distinctive reality of Christianity as all that Christianity is. It encourages living in the meanings of the faith, simply avoiding any implication that these are universal meanings. It turns away from the quest to understand Christianity from a transcendent perspective toward immersion within the faith itself. The church ceases to try to explain itself to others in a language familiar to them, and simply lives its own faith.

III

There can be little doubt that of the three options I have sketched, the third is the most promising for the church. It authorizes the church to do its business. Indeed, it frees the church from many distractions to concentrate on its own internal worship and corporate life. This does not exclude social action in the wider community, but that action is to flow out of the church's own understanding as shaped by its own language, not from a secular theory. Surely, this has much to commend it.

Nevertheless, I am not satisfied with this proposal, and I am quite skeptical that it can work in practice. With respect to many ideas, people want to know whether they are true, and the answer that they are Christian does not entirely satisfy. There is in Christianity a thrust toward self-transcendence and self-criticism, so that the confidence that certain things have been asserted in the past, even in the Bible, is often the beginning of the discussion rather than the end. Not everyone is so curious; so the approach will work for some. But I would regret the loss of those among whom the principle of self-criticism is better developed, and indeed I would be one of those who are lost.

The usual answer to this objection of mine is that it is naive, that there is no way of asking about truth outside a cultural-linguistic system. There is no metasystem in terms of which the affirmations of each can be judged. Those who ask about the truth of Christian language, as if there were some higher court of appeal, it is argued, have not yet understood that language. In this view, the task is not to answer questions of truth, but to show that when one understands language properly, such questions do not arise.

These questions do not arise, for advocates of this proposal, because Christian affirmations are no longer understood to refer to any objective state of affairs. The meaning of each statement is found in its relation to others and to the pattern of corporate life that is associated with the language as a whole. Questions about the reality of God do not arise, because the meaning of asserting God's reality is exhausted in the way the use of that word is related to the use of other words in the Christian symbol system and to the way people act in relation to its use.

My own opinion is that this strategy cannot succeed. The pattern of behavior associated with the use of these words arose in a period when no one doubted that they referred to objective reality. Believers may have been wrong, but the belief that God existed quite independently of their language and behavior was essential to shaping that language and behavior. Many intellectuals have learned, since the rise of various forms of idealism and language philosophy, to stifle questions about the independent reality of God, but even they find it hard to be consistent. I do not anticipate that ordinary believers will follow suit.

IV

I have outlined three traditions and their current outcomes. I did not take time to criticize the final forms of the first two because, insofar as they are different from the third, they offer little promise for the church. The first relativizes in a way that inevitably depreciates the riches of the tradition, whatever the intention may be. The second objectifies the many religions, viewing them all, including Christianity, from the outside. The third, on the other hand, affirms the full richness of Christian language and liturgy and provides a basis for the church to understand itself and enter into a rich internal life. It is because it is attractive that I have called attention to its limitations. The question I now want to address is whether there is a better way for Christianity to understand itself while recognizing that it is one religious tradition among others. Specifically, can we renew Christian claims to universality without returning to the arrogant and oppressive role that has characterized Christianity in the past?

I believe we can. But this will require that we think of diverse religious traditions and their claims in a fresh way.

Generally, when people encounter highly divergent movements, they suppose that these are compatible with one another, that, if one is right or true, the others must be wrong or false. In reaction against that, others often move to a radically relativistic position, accepting each in its own terms and denying that there is any perspective from which they can be evaluated objectively. In describing the present scene, it is this relativistic position that I have been discussing thus far. But I believe there is another and better option.

Imagine with me, if you will, that the totality of what is, is very complex, far exceeding all that we can ever hope to know or think. Now suppose that in different parts of the world at different times, remarkable individuals have penetrated into this reality and discovered features of it that are really there to be found. In some instances, what they learn is merely of intellectual interest, but often it has profound meaning for the way life should be lived. The insight may be into nature, into history, or into what transcends nature and history alike.

Many times, presumably, these insights have died with those who attained them. But in other cases, they were shared, and communities of people developed around what was learned. They have worked out the implications of their respective insights for thought and practice, and they have developed institutions to preserve and carry on what was being discovered. Sometimes, further insights emerged in this process and the traditions have received major new stimuli.

When I speak of insights, I imply that something has been seen that is really there to be seen. When I speak of working out their implications, I assume that these implications also have their truth. But all the expressions of the insights and of their implications are also shaped by cultural and historical factors that may illumine, but also may distort. I assume, further, that those who are most eager to defend the new truth are likely to see differing ideas and claims as dangerous to it, and to oppose them, whether or not they directly and necessarily conflict.

But now suppose that times change and that heirs of these several traditions meet and converse in friendly ways, genuinely curious about one another. The fact of the difference now does not necessarily mean that they should reject and oppose one another. It may be that the differing insights out of which they have developed their contrasting and conflicting systems are all true! If so, they all have much to learn.

Finding out whether representatives of one community can accept particular ideas important to another is a very difficult task. Initial formulations usually suggest that this is impossible. Consider an example. Christians have a deep appreciation for the personal self. At the heart of Buddhist teaching is the doctrine of no-self, the denial that there is a personal self. Surely, if we do not adopt a complete relativism of the sort I am opposing, we must say that only one can be correct! The other must be flatly wrong.

Yet, those Christians who have engaged in dialogue with Buddhists know that we are not reduced to such alternatives. We listen attentively to Buddhists explaining their no-self doctrine. We think long and hard about what is at the heart of our prizing of the personal self. We find many of the points made by Buddhists congenial to ideas of unselfishness and selflessness that have played a role in our own tradition. We recognize that all too often our talk of the personal self has been bound up with philosophical and psychological doctrines that, on reflection, we do not see to be necessary to our Christian faith. Step by step, this process leads us to openness to what the Buddhist is saying. On the other hand, the Buddhist may see that the deepest Christian reason for affirming the personal self does not need to be flatly opposed. Eventually, at least for some of the participants, a view of self emerges that is different from either the historic Christian one or the traditional Buddhist formulation: one that affirms the central insights of both without the mutual negations.

This does not guarantee the complete truth of the new belief. But in my view, a belief that contains two distinct insights is closer to the truth than one that affirms one insight to the exclusion of the other. Something may be lost, but the likelihood is strong that more is gained.

Now suppose that Christians, having reformulated our beliefs so as to take account of Buddhist insights, have the opportunity to interact extensively with Native Americans. They, too, have insights into human existence, for example, into the way it is related to the earth. Initially, what is heard will seem very different from the Buddhist-Christian anthropology resulting from the previous encounter, even contradictory. But with sufficient patience and good will, there is a real chance that ways will be found to do some measure of justice to the deepest insights of Native Americans without giving up either our Christian insights or the Buddhist ones.

I do not mean to suggest that all Christians can devote themselves to endless conversations with persons from other traditions. Christians have other things to do. But if the relation among the beliefs of the many traditions is of this sort, then we do not need to relativize our beliefs. Quite the contrary. We can believe that our own tradition is rich in insights, insights that are true not only for us but for all. This is my central point. We can affirm our insights as universally valid! What we cannot do, without lapsing back into unjustified arrogance, is to deny that the insights of other traditions also are universally valid.

Of course, the awareness that heirs of other traditions have universally valid insights to share with us alters the way we think about our own. We will systematically free ourselves from the sort of universal claims that explicitly or implicitly assert that others have nothing to teach us. We will accent within our own heritage those teachings that point to the future as the time when the fullness of truth will be manifest, and we will tone down those statements that seem to imply that we already have the fullness of truth. Our tradition offers us ample resources for making these moves.

At present, church bodies often acknowledge that they can learn from one another, but they seem to be afraid to admit that Christians can also learn from other religious traditions. This is a sad commentary on the quality of our trust in God and openness to the Spirit who is to lead us into all truth. It expresses our resistance to learn from the New Testament the strength of weakness. Real strength lies not in clinging to what we have already received, but in openness to learn from others. Such openness does not mean that we despise what we now know or think that we should wait for more before we act on the light we already have. Paul knew that he saw through a glass darkly, but this did not discourage him from speaking with conviction about what he saw. Indeed, what we already know should make us eager to learn more and to grow into a fuller truth. It is the strength of our biblical convictions that presses us toward the fuller truth that is to come.

V

My argument thus far is that we Christians have truths about humanity, about nature, and about God that are universally valid. We should not be hesitant to claim them and share them. We should shape our lives by them and encourage others to do the same. But we should understand that those truths are but a small part of the whole truth, that we need the help of others in advancing toward that whole, that we should honor the universality of their messages as well. In that spirit, we could renew conviction and commitment in our churches. Perhaps we could even persuade our children that something important is going on there, something in which they would want to participate. Perhaps the wider public would begin to look to the church as a place from which it could expect creative thinking and helpful guidance in the confusion of a relativistic world.

I am letting myself be carried away. In fact, the church is resisting this move. Its leadership seems more comfortable celebrating its particularity in accustomed ways than claiming its universality, if that claim requires change. It is easy to interpret this resistance as inertia and defensiveness, and surely these human weaknesses play a role. But is there more? Are there theological reasons for opposing the adventure on which I would like to see the church embark?

It may be that the deepest resistance centers around the understanding of Christ. Christians believe that Christ is the Way, the Truth, and the Life. We understand that to mean that Christ is all-sufficient. To many, it seems that if we acknowledge that other traditions have universal truths that we need to learn from them, then we are denying Christ or viewing Christ as but one teacher among others, rather than as the savior of the world. In the name of Christ, we are self-protective and close ourselves to others.

But is this biblically and theologically the deepest meaning of Christ? Are not defensiveness and closedness to truth strange modes of faithfulness to Christ? Are they not, finally, incompatible with radical faith, which surely includes if it does not simply mean, radical trust? Is there not a better way of understanding Christ?

I believe there is. I do truly believe that Christ is the Way, and that living the Way is of supreme importance in every generation, but above all today. What is that Way? It is the Way of Truth and Life, of faith, hope, and love. Still more concretely, what does that mean? The chief point is to choose between two images of the Way. One is the image of following a blueprint already given, or fitting our lives to a fixed set of guidelines. This is the way of legalism. The second image is that of trusting the Spirit that leads us into all truth, responding to opportunities as they arise, relating to our neighbors in love, opening ourselves to individual and collective criticism, testifying to the truth we have and seeking to learn more. This, I believe, is the way that is Christ. Having begun with the Spirit, why do we turn back to the law—oh, we of little faith!

But with all my talk of the Spirit and the living Christ, am I neglecting the historical figure of Jesus and the claim he has upon us? I do not think so. I think that my talk of Christ and the Spirit is quite continuous with the message of Jesus and of his cross and resurrection. He did not lay out a practical guide for future conduct in the church. Where he was original and creative as a teacher, his role was to break open his hearers, to let them be transformed. The Way he embodied and offered was one of being open to surprise and new perceptions, not of clinging to established guidelines and inherited patterns. The early church's message of a crucified Messiah likewise was a shock, breaking into deep-seated expectations and habits of thought. To think of Christ as binding us to the past, assuring us that we already know all that we need to know, encouraging us to closure, has no basis in what we know of Jesus' life, teaching, cross, and resurrection.

Or the objection may be that I am neglecting the great creeds of the church. Some think that the Christian doctrine of incarnation requires that we claim an exclusive uniqueness for ourselves that prevents us from accepting the truth that others have found. Bur surely this is not the case! It was not the case in the early church. The conviction that Jesus was the incarnation of the Logos opened many of the church's leading thinkers to believe that the same Logos that was incarnate in

Jesus also spoke through the wisest of the Greeks. The church, in fact, internalized many insights of Aristotle, Plato, Polinus, and the Stoics.

But perhaps the inclusion of Greek ideas in the development of Christian thought was a great mistake. Perhaps we should have understood the doctrine of incarnation to mean that all truth is to be found exclusively in Jesus, that we are to defend the biblical faith by ignoring all else or treating all else in ignorance and error. We have some basis in the Reformers for moving in that direction. Perhaps my proposal involves the abandonment of the greatest insights of the Protestant tradition.

Again, I do not think so. The true insight of Luther was that major insights of the Bible had been obscured in the process of hellenization. What was most important in his time was the recovery of those insights. In his impassioned work on their behalf, he often overspoke himself in his condemnation of others. To follow Luther rightly is not to adopt straightforwardly his attacks on the papacy, the nobility, the peasants, the Jews, Erasmian humanism, philosophy, reason, and the Epistle of James. It is to learn from him the importance of listening to the Bible openly and honestly, even when its word does not fit our expectation and preference, and to find in it, above all, the message of grace.

The Reformers can help us in another respect as well. They can free us from bondage to Greek formulations of Christian beliefs. Those who resist learning from Buddhists, or from representatives of primal communities, often, without realizing it, base their resistance not on biblical insights but on Greek thought. For example, it has been hellenized thought, much more than biblical teaching itself, that has made it difficult to accept the insight in the Buddhist doctrine of no-self. This does not mean that in our eagerness to learn from Buddhists, we should lose the insights we have gained from the Greeks. But it may help us in the process of honing the formulations of our present beliefs, to recognize how often we have confused the biblical insights with their hellenized expression. Truly, to recognize that what we know as Chritianity is a hellenized, and subsequently modernized, form may enable us to open ourselves to Buddhized and primalized forms as well, and to look for the fullness of truth through all and beyond all.

Let me finally say directly what I mean by "Christ." I mean the incarnation of God in the world. That God is in the world, and the effect God's presence has in the world, we know in and through Jesus. The way God was present in him was unique. But Christ is not limited to the one historical person. When Paul spoke of the Christian life as being "in Christ" he could not have said, with identical meaning, "in Jesus." Christ was alive in the church. The church was, or could be, a continuing incarnation of God, the body of Christ. God is incarnate in the world as well. Our task is to discern Christ in our neighbor and to see what Christ is doing in the world today, to join in that work, and to let Christ be in us as well.

I am affirming that God is present in the world at all times and places, that we Christians know this presence as Christ, that Christ is the creative, redemptive, life-giving power in the world. Those are strong, universal affirmations. Do they return us to the arrogant, exclusivistic, and oppressive theology from which it is so important to separate ourselves?

They need not, and they must not. To affirm the truth of God's universal presence arrogantly, exclusivistically, and oppressively is to falsify it. It is to turn good news into bad news. To avoid that, we must think through, and learn to articulate, the crucial point, which is that the truth of this universal assertion by Christians does not exclude the truth of the universally relevant insights of others.

Consider the Buddhist claim that Gautama is the Buddha. That is a very different statement form the assertion that God was incarnate in Jesus. The Buddha is the one who is enlightened. To be enlightened is to realize the fundamental nature of reality, its insubstantiality, its relativity, its emptiness. To realize that is to be liberated from all attachment and all illusion, and to live in perfect compassion. This enlightenment is in principle open to all. But what enlightenment really is, that is made known in and through Gautama.

I hope my point is clear. The Buddhist claim is extremely different from the Christian one. It is based on very different interests and very different insights. Many doctrines that have been developed in support of these different insights are in conflict. But the basic insights themselves do not contradict one another. That Jesus was the incarnation of God does not deny that Gautama was the Enlightened One. In that vast complexity that is all that is, it may well be that God works creatively in all things and that at the same time, in the Buddhist sense, all things are empty. Perhaps we will understand God's creative and redemptive presence better when we also understand that all things are relative and insubstantial. Indeed, I believe that is the case. To affirm both that Jesus is the Christ and that Gautama is the Buddha is to move our understanding closer to the truth. To learn from some primal people that the earth is alive, that human beings are her children, that in wounding her we wound ourselves as well will carry us still further toward the truth.

Learning from others in this way certainly requires *extensive* rethinking of our received faith. That is the task of theology in every generation. But such thinking does not threaten or relativize our faith. It is because of our faith that we open ourselves to others, and the resultant growth is at once in understanding and in faith. Our confidence in the universality of Christ grows as we live in Christ, and living in Christ—that is, trusting the creative and redemptive work of God—expands the horizons of our understanding.

VI

I speak with pain and passion. We live in a time when the world needs Christ as never before. We are all lost, and Christ is the Way. I think I see what it would mean to follow that Way, to trust Christ, to be led by Christ toward all truth. I think it would mean once again knowing the life that is so hard to discern in churches now.

I see us, instead, trying to decide between two options, both deadly. One is to relativize our faith and, with it, Christ, abandoning confidence in the universal saving power that is the Way, the Truth, and the Life. The other is to identify Christ with past forms of the tradition that we now know to have been profoundly oppressive.

I fear that we are already far down the paths that lead to death. But today, again, God sets before us the great choice, the choice between death and life. May we hear once more the words of Moses as reported in Deuteronomy: "Therefore choose life." And may we obey!

6

Can Christ Become Good News Again?

In my youth I had a number of doubts about Christianity. There were questions about the virgin birth and the bodily resurrection. There were questions about life after death and what happened to those who did not believe. There were questions about free will and predestination. But there was no question in my mind about the goodness of Jesus Christ. There was no question but that the Christian message was good news.

My work as a student at the University of Chicago raised more fundamental questions. Whether the Christian message was fundamentally true became for me a matter of deep uncertainty. I became unsure whether the word "God" had any positive meaning or reference. My faith was in tatters. But even then, I did not doubt that Christ would be good news—if only the news were true. Thus, even in my doubts, I remained, from our present perspective, profoundly innocent. I shared that innocence with many of my generation.

I do not mean that we were unaware that much evil had been done in the name of Christ. In my childhood, I had been taught to be shocked by the Crusades and the Inquisition. We tended to associate those with Roman Catholicism, but we knew that the Reformers also

The address delivered by Dr. Cobb at the retirement luncheon in his honor, at the School of Theology at Claremont, November 1989.

had committed their share of crimes. We knew of the appalling destructiveness of the religious wars and that we Protestants did not have clean hands. Hence, I do not want to exaggerate our innocence. But in our minds, Christianity as such, and certainly Christ, remained essentially good, despite the evil that had been committed in their names.

Looking back on the period after the end of World War II, it is hard to see how such innocence was possible. We were somewhat aware of the horrors that the Nazis had inflicted on the Jews, and of course we knew, vaguely, of pogroms and persecutions in earlier periods. But none of that seemed to have much to do with Christianity or with Christ. Since Nazism was anti-Christian, we thought it was not reasonable for Christianity to be blamed. And we associated the persecution of Jews by Christians with medieval intolerance rather than with Christianity in general.

It has been only quite gradually, as the result of persistent work by a handful of Jewish and Christian writers, that we have come to see the Holocaust as the outcome of Christian teaching as well as of particular twists given this by anti-Christian Nazis. We have been forced to see that the anti-Jewish teaching that culminated in this evil has been central, not peripheral, to Christian teaching throughout most of Christian history, that it is present already in the New Testament itself. True, one can hardly picture the Jewish rabbi, Jesus, as himself anti-Jewish, but from the beginning of Christianity, his role has been depicted as discrediting Judaism and superseding it.

All this has been deeply painful for us as Christians to assimilate. It has been for me especially painful to begin provisionally to look at Christ through Jewish eyes, and to see how symbols such as the cross, so precious to me, have appeared as images of destruction and persecution to Jews. For Jews, Christ has been bad news, and despite all the advances in Christian penitence for Christian anti-Judaism, we must acknowledge that, overall and in general, Christ remains bad news for Jews today. In our own country, it seems to be secularization more than Christian faith that has brought a large measure of relief to Jews.

In the years after World War II, the history of Christian missions could still be taught in basically affirmative, even enthusiastic, ways. The genuine heroism of many missionaries could be celebrated. Of course, the connection between missions and imperialism, in Africa, for example, was not hidden from us. But is was still possible to point to the ways in which Christianity moderated the onslaughts of colonial governments and provided humanizing institutions. As the former colonies became independent, it was possible to rejoice in the new role of the missions in preparing the leaders of the newly independent nations. With all our awareness of the evils of colonialism, the sense of the positive value of Western civilization was such that we could think of contributions as well as losses from colonialism itself. By associating Christianity with the most positive aspects of the Western impact on Africa, by emphasizing, for example, its contribution to the spread of independence across the continent, it was possible to attribute to Christ an affirmative role.

Gradually, we have come to realize that this positive evaluation of Christian missions in Africa has been bound up with an unjust and unrealistic appraisal of the quality of life on that continent prior to the impact of the West. It was true that many of the peoples of Africa had not possessed the particular benefits of Western culture until these were forced upon them, but their own traditional culture had been profoundly humanizing in many ways. It included patterns of living among themselves and with nature that were considerably superior to what resulted from European dominance. We came to realize that not only the colonialists, but also the missionaries had been blind to the values of the ancient culture, and that perhaps it was Christians above all who, in their zeal to help, did most to destroy it.

We see now that even the medicine of which we Westerners are so proud has been at best highly ambiguous in its effects, leading to a population explosion that threatens to impoverish the whole continent. We see that the educational system we took to Africa educated people away from their communities, impoverishing these communities and developing an alienated class. We see that the application of Western agricultural practices has, in fact, led to the replacement of sustainable agriculture with methods that are expanding deserts and losing topsoil at an altogether unsustainable rate. It is hard to say that Christ has been good news for Africa!

In my youth and early adulthood, I thought that among the great achievements of Christianity was its celebration of the infinite worth of every human being. Whereas for peoples who had not been shaped by the Bible, I thought, human life was cheap, Christians knew that every person is a child of God. Despite all our failures to live up to our beliefs, I saw this affirmation of each individual as having gradually expressed itself in democracy and in human rights. This appeared to me then as an unqualified gain.

Only very slowly, beginning in the late sixties, did I realize that there was a dark side to this as well. Christianity has, no doubt, encouraged the emergence of strong individuals, but this has been accompanied by the rise of an individualism that has been destructive of community. Even more clearly, the emphasis on the infinite worth of every human being has been closely connected with the idea that all the rest of creation exists only as means to our human ends.

I do not wish to belittle the positive value of the preoccupation with issues of human justice that has characterized the progressive elements in world Christianity since World War II. But it has been sad to watch the resistance of Christians to taking seriously the destruction of our planet. We have been far from the lead in these matters, often criticizing those who *have* taken the lead, for distracting attention from *our* issues. Now at last, as environmental problems dominate the headlines of our newspapers, we have recognized that this resistance is not supported by our scriptures. Finally, we are willing to admit that, where changes in the environment threaten human beings, we should call attention to them and urge action to slow down destructive practices. But we are hardly yet willing to acknowledge that this destruction is evil even apart from its effects on us. Our anthropocentrism still resists recognizing the intrinsic importance of the nonhuman world. For that reason, we remain in the rear guard of the environmental movement. Christ has not been good news for the environment and those who care about it.

This has been particularly manifest with regard to issues of human treatment of other animals. Especially in our century, the widespread assumption that other animals exist only for human use and enjoyment has been acted out on a vast scale. Five hundred million animals a year die, usually after much suffering, to test cosmetics, provide examples for study, or to advance science. Farm animals now rarely lead natural lives. They are treated more and more as factory products, and the resulting suffering is extreme. Now they are begin transformed by biotechnology with no regard to the misery of the newly created species—if only they provide more meat at lower cost. But despite the fact that many of our secular neighbors have responded in moral outrage to our cruelty to other animals, the church has remained silent to this day. Apparently, from a Christian point of view, the suffering of our fellow creatures is a matter of indifference. Christ is bad news for animals.

In the seventies, in this country, the strongest voice of protest against Christian teaching and action came from liberated women who are seeking to clarify the sources of their age-long oppression. Few would say that Christianity initiated this oppression, and fewer still would single out Jesus as particularly guilty of enforcing it. But many point out that the Bible as a whole is patriarchal to the core.

Further, this is not really a reflection of the universal patriarchal character of its environment. It is also a matter of systematically affirming patriarchy where this was softened by religious practices and teachings of others. In this sense, Judaism, Christianity, and Islam are patriarchal religions by choice and intention. Since Christianity has been the greatest agent for spreading this patriarchal religion around the world, the Christ to whom it witnesses cannot be good news to women!

Through the years, Christ has represented "high moral standards" in the area of sex. For much of Christian history, this has meant restricting sex as much as possible and favoring celibacy. Sex has been identified with the flesh that is at war with the spirit, and Christianity has called for its repression. Millions have suffered personally as a result, and the resultant preoccupation with sex has distorted the collective psyche of Christendom.

To some extent this epoch has passed. The sexual revolution that arose in protest against Christian teaching has penetrated the churches and forced a reconsideration of the healthier attitudes toward sexuality in the Bible. The view of sexuality as unclean, which dominated Christian teaching through most of our history, is on the defensive. The church is still profoundly confused, but the many centuries in which Christ represented the repression of the body are coming to an end. Christ is ceasing to be bad news in this important respect.

But there is as yet one major exception. Although women in general have suffered under patriarchy as the major object of oppression, they have at least been assigned a crucial role within it. Patriarchy has found ways of persuading them to cooperate in their oppression. But there is another group who has no role in patriarchal society at all, and who receives no protection within it. These are homosexuals.

Today the churches are conceding to women a place in the sun. There is some measure of repentance for the millenia-long oppression sanctioned by the church's teaching and enforced by its practice. But against homosexuals, the church continues to appeal to elements of patriarchal morality embedded in its scriptures and thoroughly articulated in its later teaching. Some concession is now made to the effect that having desire for persons of the same sex may not in itself be sinful. But it is still asserted that to act on that desire is immoral. Hence, a homosexual, to satisfy the demands of the patriarchal church, must either abstain from sexual activity throughout life or "convert" to heterosexual behavior. Christ is certainly bad news for homosexual persons.

If Christ is bad news to all these groups, can Christ still be good new to others? The answer is no! For Christ to be good news to any, Christ must be good news to all. Universality is an indispensable element in the good news bound up with Christ. Hence, the title of my lecture. It implies that once Christ was good news. We realize now that we were wrong in thinking that Christ was good news to all, and in that realization Christ ceases to be good news for us as well. The question now is "Can Christ become good news again?"

The future of Christianity hangs in the balance. That does not mean that Christianity will come to an end if a positive answer cannot be found in the face of the new awareness of how Christ has been bad news for many. Far from it. But those who are aware of, and who have been sensitized by Christ to care for, the suffering and the oppressed will not be able to give themselves to the service of Christ wholeheartedly. Most of them will distance themselves from Christianity, leaving the churches to those who are still innocent, willfully blind, or willing to serve in partisan spirit a "Christ" who is the enemy of many. The inner check against idolatry, which has been so important in the history of Christianity, will grow weak. Christ will become increasingly bad news to the world.

Should we then abandon Christ? Certainly many have done so, and others are doing so every day. But the ancient question of the disciples then comes to us. To whom should we go? Most of those who turn away from Christ, today, turn toward the secular gods of economic success, social acceptance, and the good life as defined in Yuppiedom. Others, more thoughtfully and wisely, turn to the ancient religious traditions of southern and eastern Asia. Some women seek a new spirituality, largely disconnected from any of the patriarchal traditions that have shaped civilization. Still other former Christians search in lonely isolation for a way of being in the world authentically.

I do not intend in this lecture to discuss these and other options. Ours is a day in which the spiritual quest must be pursued in many directions, since our heritage, as it now exists, does not serve us well. I am quite sure that none of the options are free from problems, and it is my personal belief that none have the full range of potential of a repentant Christianity. In any case, none are real options for me. I *am* a Christian, and my vocation is to participate in Christian repentance rather than to leave the church to those who see no need to repent. So I ask once more, can Christ become good news again?

The truth is that, for me, the "Christ" who is bad news is not Christ at all. This points to the necessity of clarifying what I have been meaning by "Christ." With such a powerful word, that is no easy task.

"Christ" is the central image of Christian faith. Thus, what it conveys is a cluster of meanings conditioned by all that Christians take to be most precious and most normative. Its meaning is profoundly shaped by the memory of Jesus, but it does not function simply as a name or title for that man. It also refers to God, as God has come to be known through Jesus and as incarnate in him. Sometimes the accent is on Jesus as the one in whom God was incarnate. Sometimes the accent is on God's present activity in the world as that is conditioned by, and understood through, Jesus. Less often, the reference is to those who now embody that present activity of God in ways that are peculiarly reminiscent of Jesus. Sometimes we call them "Christs" or "Christ-figures."

There is for Christian believers no appeal beyond Christ. There is no higher calling than to trust and serve Christ. One cannot appeal from Christ to God, since "Christ" names God as Christians have come to know God through Jesus. Christians as Christians cannot acknowledge some other, truer revelation. If one appeals against Christ to some rational principle or natural law, one has, to that extent, ceased to be a believer. One may well, in the name of Christ, seek wisdom and truth in many sources, and as a result one may come to a new, transformed understanding of Christ. But if one appeals to this other wisdom and truth as a way of relativizing the truth and wisdom that is in Christ, to that extent one is not acting as a believer. For the believer as believer, there cannot be a standard of truth and goodness beyond Christ.

Hence, when I say that we now see that, for many, Christ has been bad news, I mean that the whole cluster of beliefs and practices thought by Christians to be ideal has worked against the well-being of these people and groups. This is quite distinct from the fact that Christians in every generation have failed to live up to their norms and have, as a result, committed every kind of evil. I have not been talking about the behavior of Christians that they themselves recognize as sin or as unavoidable compromise with the world. I have been talking about what Christians have done when they have been truest to their own teachings. It has often been wholehearted Christians, sometimes those whom we have canonized as saints, from whom Jews have learned to expect the worst. For many centuries, Jews were able to survive in Christendom more because many rulers were willing to compromise their Christian ideals for practical purposes than because of those ideals themselves.

Now I am saying that for me the "Christ" who has been bad news for so many is not truly Christ at all. What does that mean? It means that part of the deepest meaning of "Christ," not only now but also throughout history, is "good news to all." That element in its meaning has often been subordinated to other elements. That subordination remains prominent in the churches today. But the note of good news has not disappeared. And when Christians recognize that the other elements have been so structured as to destroy this one, this recognition at least introduced discomfort for most Christians. We see that something is wrong. The "Christ" we have served cannot be the true Christ.

Of course, our first reaction is to deny that Christ has been bad news, or at least that the Christ *we* now serve is bad news. We claim that the problem lies elsewhere, for example, that the refusal of others to accept our good news is the reason that it appears to them as bad news. Or we claim that, if all would accept the Christ we proclaim, the other problems I have noted would take care of themselves. It is only after all these defenses and escapes are exposed and undercut that we are forced to admit that the Christ we have trusted and served, understood just as we have understood, is for many bad news, and hence also bad news for us. It is only then that we are willing to ask, "Can Christ become good news again?"

One strategy suggested by that question is to see whether we can discover any norm, teaching, insight, way of being in all the world, or life-orientation that *would* be good news for all. In the days when there was more confidence in being able to describe "the human condition," that seemed possible. For example, if the human condition is one of sin and guilt, then forgiveness and cleansing are good news to all. But we have found that what Christians mean by sin is not a universal condition, or at least that it is not felt to be a fundamental feature of human existence in all cultures. In that situation, if the message of forgiveness requires that first we compel people to acknowledge their sinfulness, it is not unqualified good news! The result is the same if we begin instead with alienation. People in many cultures, especially primal ones, have not experienced themselves as alienated. If our good news is a response to alienation, then they can receive it as such only after we have alienated them from their own cultures. This is not unqualified good news either!

In our pluralistic age, we must inquire whether we have been asking the question in the right way. We have thought that our good news was news that all should receive as such. But just this need to share our good news, and to persuade others to accept it, has made it bad news to many, regardless of the content. Jews, especially, seek to preserve their identity against all odds. The persuasiveness of Christianity is, for them, bad news, and for Christianity to take a form that is free from its historic anti-Judaism would only compound this aspect of the problem. Perhaps our good news can only be good news to all when it ceases to contain within itself the impulse to impose itself on others, or if it can be heard and acknowledged by others without any concomitant pressure upon them to become part of the Christian community.

Would it be possible, by including this pluralistic understanding, so to formulate the essence of Christianity that it would at once be good news to all the groups I have mentioned, and to everyone else as well? Perhaps, but I doubt it. And if we did succeed, we can be sure that, as the situation changes, the essence as defined by us would not seem appropriate to the next generation. The quest for an essence is connected with a static view of reality. It is a fundamentally unhistorical approach. Christianity is a historical movement, and although much remains the same, generation after generation, we cannot now determine what will change in the future. Efforts to identify the changeless essence a generation or two ago could not foresee the changes that have been brought about by feminist and ecological insights, and in fact they were largely blind to the evils of Christian anti-Judaism as well. Even if now we were fully conscientized on all these matters, there would be no reason to think that we had become free from blindness on others.

To me, it has seemed better to focus on the way change occurs rather than on the specific content at any given time. Much change is destructive. There are changes going on in American Protestant Christianity today that, I believe, are profoundly dangerous. There are other changes that seem to me healthy and necessary. I want to affirm the latter changes as faithful to Christ, and to declare the former ones unfaithful. But how can this be done in any way other than by simply juxtaposing my prejudices against those of others?

It will be best to give examples. Within oldline Protestant Christianity today, there is an attempt to renew the effort to convert people in other countries from whatever faith they now have to Christianity, and specifically to incorporate them in the denomination of the missionaries. Some of those who are pushing for renewed zeal in this endeavor also are calling for the effort to convert Jews, an effort abandoned by the oldline denominations some time ago. I do not myself oppose all missionary effort to convert people to our churches, but I believe each case should be considered on its own merits. The proposal that we return to the effort to convert everyone who is not now Christian to one or another of our churches is one that I do not now find faithful to Christ, especially when it includes Jews among the people to be converted.

There is, on the other hand, a movement of rethinking the Christian faith, and its whole range of teaching, in light of what past embodiments of faith have done to Jews. When this approach is taken, we are required to listen extensively and intensively to Jews, to learn their needs and how our projects have interfered with their realization of their goals. We certainly need not be uncritical of them as they criticize us, but our primary task is to listen and to change ourselves so that we cease to be destructive in our relation to them.

Here are two proposed changes, both claiming to be faithful to Christ. Surely an important theological task is to reflect on how we can most faithfully decide between them. The argument for the former is that it takes biblical and traditional teachings seriously, and seeks to apply them consistently to current church practice. In the Gospel according to Matthew, we are told to go throughout the world, making disciples of all people. The consistent deduction from those instructions is that we should make disciples of Jews, too, also today. If we believe that there is no salvation apart from faith in Jesus Christ, then our failure to preach the gospel to Jews, far from showing love to them, is in fact a betrayal of our responsibility to them. The method here is that of deducing current teaching and practice from long-established doctrines held to be essential to the faith.

The argument for the second proposal is quite different. It stems from the realization that deducing teaching and practice from earlier doctrines has led to immense evil as well as to immense good. As we realize this, our commitment to Christ calls us to repentance. To repent means not merely being sorry for our share in the persecution of Jews, but also transforming who we are, so that we will no longer contribute to Jewish suffering. To do that well requires seeing the world through Jewish eyes, an act of empathy that is central to love. We can move even provisionally in this direction only as we listen non-defensively to what Jews have to say to us. Thus, the method here is to listen to what in the past we have not heard, internalize it, and rethink our heritage in light of it. Out of that, we can expect quite new teachings and quite new practices to emerge.

Now, let us ask again, which of these directions of change is most faithful to Christ? If we ask, "Which will be understood as good news by Jews?" there can be no question but that the second option wins. But the first is premised on the belief that we have a knowledge as to what is truly good for Jews that they do not share, and that we have the responsibility to act accordingly. It has on its side explicit New

Testament texts as well as a long history of their interpretation and application. From its own perspective, it does not seek to change Christianity; it seeks to renew faithfulness to its unchanging essence.

The second is premised on the belief that obedience to Christ is not primarily a matter of applying New Testament texts straightforwardly to present situations. Historical change is real, and obedience to Christ calls for rethinking the faith in light of that change. When the Great Commission was given, there had been no millenia-long Christian persecution of Jews. To apply it today, as if that persecution had not occurred, is unfaithful to Christ. To be faithful to Christ is to embody today the love that Jesus displayed in his time, and that the early Christian community carried forward. Today, that love must express itself in openness to those to whom we have spoken so long without listening. To be open in this way is to internalize what before was external, and that means to be transformed in unpredictable ways.

There can be no final proof that one response is more truly faithful to Christ than the other. At some point, we must simply confess our own faith. Certainly an unchanged Christianity that repeats the patterns of the past will not be experienced as good news by any of the groups of which I have spoken. As one for whom Christ is not truly Christ when the message of Christ and the embodiment of Christ are experienced by others as bad news, it is obvious where I must come down. Faithfulness to Christ means openness to those we have hurt, and willingness to be transformed as we listen to them. In fact, it also involves openness to all who have a word of truth and wisdom to share with us. It involves a continual process of repentance, since we are continually prone to treat the understanding we have as more final than it really is, and to defend it against points of view and insights that threaten our security in it.

Faithfulness to Christ does not lead us to lack of appreciation for what we have received from our Christian past. Quite the contrary. But it does lead us to acknowledge that the fullness of truth lies in the future and requires the contributions of all for its attainment.

If Christ comes to mean for Christians not so much a particular set of beliefs and practices as a way of being in the world that is open to what others have to say and ready to change as it learns from them, then, I think, Christ can be good news to Jews, to Africans, to our fellow creatures, to women, and to homosexuals—indeed, to all. Christ will be good news in two ways. For those who have suffered from Christianity, there will be the assurance that those who live in Christ will cease to impose themselves, demanding agreement and conformity, and will instead listen and learn. But Christ will also be good news in that many who are not Christian will find that the way of being in the world symbolized by, and embodied in, Christ is healing and fulfilling for them as well. The acceptance of this Christ need not involve the abandonment of the truth and wisdom of their own traditions or even abandonment of traditional culture and community. It can mean, instead, participation in the creative transformation of their own cultures and communities.

I know, from long experience, that there is much resistance to this shift in the way of understanding Christ. It is because I think it so important that I am addressing it again in this retirement lecture. We need a liberating Christ; but Christ cannot liberate unless Christ is liberated from the baggage that has made Christ, for so many, the oppressor. If the church clings to that baggage, the future, not only for the church but also for the planet, is bleak. So let me try to respond to some of the objections. In the process, I hope my own proposal will become clearer.

One objection is that connecting Christ with a particular pattern of change seems to deny to Christian faith its distinctive history and content. In part, this objection shows that I have not communicated my meaning. The Christian movement is one whose center is Jesus Christ and which, through that center, is heir of the earlier history of Israel. It is a particular movement with a particular history. At every point in that history the church has had, and must have, innumerable specific teachings and practices. The fact that these change from generation to generation does not make them unimportant.

The church needs many concrete teachings and practices today. Our problem is not that we have too many, but that we have too few. For example, the failure of our churches to provide its children and youth with relevant, realistic, and wholesome instruction about sexuality is an astonishing and costly lacuna in their ministries. Any teaching we offer on this topic should be subject to reconsideration as new insights emerge and as society changes. But this is no reason for holding back. People need help and guidance now in dealing with the world we inhabit now. There is no need to claim infallibility in the process of providing helpful teaching and creating communities in which that teaching is put into practice. I am all for developing a Christian doctrine of sexuality today, as well as Christian doctrines on economics and politics and many other topics. But I do not want to identify Christ with these doctrines. They would constitute the best we can do today, in living and thinking in faithfulness to Christ. But just that faithfulness requires that we hold all these ideas provisionally, ready to listen to criticism and fresh insight from whatever quarter, ready also to adapt our thinking to the actual changes going on in the world.

In my opinion, we also need much fuller Christian teaching about the nature of the world in which we live, teaching informed by the best thinking in the sciences as well as by the wisdom of our heritage. I would like to see the church, once it had truly listened to what the spirits have to say, challenge them for the way their own biases distort their pronouncements, and for the way their specialized approaches fragment the understanding of the interconnected whole of God's creation. In short, for me, the identification of Christ with this mode of change, rather than with any particular doctrinal formulations or practices, liberates the church to enter into the whole range of urgent issues that confront it, not only listening, but also speaking from its own insight and wisdom, always provisionally, but not, therefore, without conviction.

A second objection is that when Christ is identified with the pattern of change rather than with content, there is no norm by which to judge the outcome of the change. This is true in one sense. To make an analogy, there is no fixed teaching or idea from which we can determine whether the conclusion of an argument is acceptable. We must instead ask whether the argument is a sound one, and whether its premises are accurate. If the answer to these questions is affirmative, then if we are rational members of the community of discourse, we must accept the conclusion even when we do not like it. The fact that it disagrees with long-cherished ideas should not lead us to reject it.

Of course, matters are never so simple. One may have a deep suspicion that one has been led astray in some way. One is likely to go back to the premises and examine them more carefully to see whether more exact formulation of what one really does believe would undercut the argument to the conclusion one resists. Even if one cannot find a way to escape the conclusion, one may retain considerable skepticism. All of this is healthy. One should not quickly surrender deep-seated convictions and intuitions the first time one finds oneself out-argued. But, on the other hand, one needs to acknowledge some failure on one's own part. One should consider what is holding one back and whether one should not let go.

The situation with the pattern of change with which I identify Christ is analogous, although in specifics, it is quite different. It is the change that occurs when Christians open themselves to the points of view of others and to insights that come from any source whatever. Of course, the Christian does not abandon her or his own convictions on this openness. On the contrary, the openness is an expression of faith in Christ, and one brings to the meeting with the other, strong beliefs that have resulted from past acts of faith. None of that is lightly set aside or even modified. But as one hears what one has not heard before, new light is sometimes shed on the whole structure of what one has believed. Everything appears somehow different. The task of rethinking and reordering all one's beliefs imposes itself on one.

The new insight may quite directly challenge some long-held and deeply meaningful conviction. It is certainly not healthy immediately to abandon what has been so precious. One should try to find a way of sharpening the new insight and the old conviction in such a fashion that they can mutually enrich rather than oppose each other. If one cannot succeed, it is still better to retain both than to cast one out. We can live with considerable confusion of this sort! But we also should recognize that this is not the last word. The goal remains the integration of the old and the new in a richer whole. There is no pre-given norm by which we can predetermine whether that whole, when it emerges, will conform to received Christian teaching. But if it is the outcome of this kind of process, then the Christian is called to live by it provisionally until a fuller understanding is possible.

There is a third objection. If individual Christians and groups of Christians develop their faith in this way, in openness to varied challenges and opportunities, there can be no assurance that there will be common elements in the outcome. Again, this is true. In fact, there can be no assurance that there are common elements in the beliefs of the many churches in the world today. What they really share is a common center in their histories, Jesus Christ. What they discover when their representatives meet in ecumenical councils is that, despite their enormous differences, this common center has led to the ability to recognize one another as Christian, and to extensive overlaps in the ways they have come to think and live. They are able to see many of their differences as complementary rather than as contradictory. They are willing to look to the future for a fuller truth that will contain the fragments of truth to which each attests now. I believe that this shows that the Christ of whom I speak has been present in all the traditions in spite of their tendency to absolutize particular positions that have emerged along the way. If they became more willing to trust Christ, and less committed to retaining their diverse traditions unchanged, mutual enrichment would be furthered and the movement toward a new unity advanced.

The fourth and final objection, of which I will speak today, is that this way of identifying Christ is too disconnected with the historical Jesus. It is true that I am not using "Christ" as a synonym for Jesus, and that one could not simply substitute "Jesus" for "Christ" in my speech. But I believe that it is precisely in Jesus that we see the transforming work of Christ most vividly manifest. The scholarship of the last generation has demonstrated that what is distinctive about Jesus' teaching is not as much a particular content as it is the way in which he challenged and broke open the deep-seated habits in the minds of his listeners. The end he sought was neither to leave the hearers shattered nor to replace with a new content all that they had previously believed. It was instead to transform the whole of their understanding and belief through the shock of new recognition.

If we turn from Jesus' own teaching to the earliest message about him, the situation is not so different. The message of the cross did not in itself provide a whole pattern of understanding to replace all that the hearers brought to their reception of the faith. On the contrary, the preaching to Jews presupposed the whole of their heritage. But the shocking word about the cross of Christ threw a different light upon the whole, and transformed its meaning. The theologies of the early church are efforts to order the new understanding that emerged from this engagement and transformation. We are not disconnected from this history when we, in our turn, are shocked out of innocence and complacency into new thinking by listening to Jews telling the history of Europe from their perspective, or women reflecting on what patriarchal civilization has been for them.

Needless to say, I have not done justice to the objections to my proposal for thinking of Christ. My purpose is to explain the proposal, not to demonstrate its superiority. My appeal, finally, is to your Christian sensibilities rather than to any objective authority.

But despite the modesty of what I have done, I believe the way of thinking to which I am pointing is urgently needed in the church. My heart is heavy as I see the abandonment of the faith by so many of those who have the most to contribute to its transformation and transmission. I grieve as I see so many of those who remain in the church seeking renewal through a return to past authorities and to ways of thinking that are now convincing only to those who do not understand the nature of our historic situation, to ways that have already proved themselves repressive of believers and oppressive of others. There is a dullness today in the denominations to which most of us belong. The struggle to survive consumes our energies and we react defensively to criticism. In our effort to find something to which we can cling, I fear that we turn Christ into an idol.

I am convinced that this suffering is self-inflicted. We need only to let go of all our idols to find again the living Christ. Christ will not guarantee us the growth of our denominations or worldly success. But to live in Christ, the true Christ, is to be free and to know the peace and joy that are so hard to discern in our churches. Christ *is* good news for us and for all. But the Christ who is good news is the spirit of life and love, the God whom we know in Jesus. Because Christ is alive, I have hope that the church will find again the good news it now obscures. Yes, Christ *can* become good news once more in our time and in our churches. That will be a miracle on the order of Vatican II and the transformation of the Soviet empire under Gorbachev. Despite all the obstacles we Christians put in Christ's way, I believe the miracle *will* happen. Christ will become good news again. May it be soon!

7

Kingdom Come and the Present Church

Although I have often taught, lectured, and spoken about the church as a theologian, I continue to have difficulty in deciding just what is at stake in theological discussion of the church. I have not resolved that problem, but I can share with you where I now am in reflecting upon it and what I have accordingly decided to do in this lecture. I begin by stating what I have decided *not* to do.

First, I have decided not to try to define the church, that is, to state what its essence is at all times and places. That may be a worthwhile effort at some times and places, and I have on occasion attempted it; but at the moment, I think it is not useful. There may not be any very significant essence in this sense. History may bring such vast changes to the church that what is important about it today may be quite different from what was important about it in the first, fifth, fifteenth, or nineteenth centuries. To find a common denominator in all times and in all those communities to which we now want to give the name church would probably provide us little guidance for the future. It

Originally delivered as part of the Thirteenth Annual Convention of the United Theological Seminary of the Twin Cities under the theme, "Rediscovering the Church." Previously published in *Theological Markings*, an occasional publication of the United Theological Seminary of the Twin Cities (Spring 1975).

might even blind us to what we are now called to become by focusing on what we have always been.

Second, I do not want to try to describe what the church factually is at the present time. Clearly, it is important for us to know as much as we can about ourselves. Sociologists and historians can tell us a great deal, and we need to be informed and judged by their contributions. We theologians can contribute to this self-description of the church because we bring to the examination questions that most sociologists and historians do not. Yet, the major task of the theologian cannot be to describe what is; ours is, in some way, a normative discipline.

Third, I do not want to formulate norms that simply express what I or others wish the church were like or would become. It has been too easy for theologians in the recent past to define ideally what it should mean to be Christian and then to judge the actual church harshly in light of this understanding; sometimes this has become a reason, or an excuse, to abandon it altogether. Those who entitled these lectures "Rediscovering the Church" may have had this phenomenon in mind. They may be suggesting that we have turned away from the church in our search for effective Christian witness and now are brought back to it by the course of events.

Instead of a definition, a description, or an ideal, I have decided to propose two images of the church. I assume these images to be Christian and to be appropriate to whatever essence the church may have, but I offer them because of their particular relevance to the situation and self-understanding of the church today. I certainly intend that they function as norms in the light of which the church should shape its present life, but just for that reason, I intend also to ground them in what the church has been and is. If these images are not already, in some fragmentary way, true of the church, then my proposals are theologically false; but the images decidedly do not arise from empirical investigation of the extant institution or community.

I

The image of the church as *the vanguard of the new age* is firmly rooted in the New Testament, and especially in Jesus' proclamation of the Kingdom. Scholars still dispute the respective roles of futurity and presentness in Jesus' understanding of the Kingdom; Rudolf Bultmann stressed futurity, whereas Norman Perrin stresses presentness. But both agree that Jesus intimately connected what was occurring in the community that gathered around him, and especially in its table fellowship, with the coming Kingdom. The disciples lived now in light of what was to come, and thereby constituted a community that already belonged to the age to come.

The sense of living from a reality other than the dominant structures and powers of their time has been characteristic of Christians throughout the centuries. Augustine described the City of God in its distinction from the worldly city. Bunyan pictured the Christian as a pilgrim on the earth where home is elsewhere. But neither of these images captured the full meaning of the coming Kingdom. Augustine associated the City of God too closely with the given institution of the church. In Bunyan, Christians reach their true home only at the end of the journey; it does not house them on their way.

In the social gospel movement, something of the original sense of the Kingdom was recovered. It was to be a new age; it was to come on earth; and the Christian found present meaning in contributing to its coming. But unlike the New Testament, the Kingdom was to be achieved by an extension of privileges already enjoyed by many. Education and democracy, for example, were to be shared with all people. There was powerful criticism of capitalism and social injustice in the movement, but the basic social institutions of family, church, school, and government were trusted as instruments for realizing the Kingdom.

In the neoorthodox and existentialist reaction against the social gospel, the tension was restored between the Kingdom and even the finest institutions of Christendom. But in the process, Christians transformed the Kingdom from an actual and hope-filled expectation into a principle of judgment upon human pretensions, whereas in the New Testament it plays this critical role only as a by-product of its positive one. Further, the new understanding of the Kingdom weakened the Christian's ability to discuss the presence of Christ in the world and limited that presence to the inner existence of the individual believer.

During the 1960s, theologians turned away from individual existence—perhaps in too sharp a reaction—toward political theology, theology of liberation, and theology of hope. For most of these, the perpendicular relation to the Kingdom has given way to a renewed sense of its futurity. They all see that the reality from which the Christian is called to live today is not found empirically or historically but only by vision, imagination, and hope. In this radical opposition of the future to the present, they differ from the theologians of the social gospel, and they more nearly recover the New Testament understanding.

The two leading theologians envision the future quite differently. Jürgen Moltmann is chiefly interested in the Christian structure of time as it prevails in every situation. Christians see the injustice in every historical situation in the light of God's promise of justice, and we identify with the oppressed in their struggles for freedom. This is what it means to live from the crucifixion and resurrection of Christ. Wolfhart Pannenberg, on the other hand, identifies Christian faith with the assurance of a final and actual coming of the Kingdom. He interprets each historical occurrence in light of its role in the universal history that leads to the consummation.

For both Moltmann and Pannenberg, the church could be viewed as the vanguard of the coming age. Both write as if this should be the normative conception of the church at all times and places. My proposal is more relativistic than this. I suggest that the rise of the future-oriented theologies reflects the concrete situation of the church today, which enables us to recover motifs from the New Testament that were inapplicable as long as Christians could interpret major extant institutions and assumptions as Christian. If a future-oriented theology succeeds in giving rise to new communities and institutions that actually do live from the future, then the appropriate image of the church will again find its analogies in later portions of the New Testament instead of in Jesus' preaching of the Kingdom. My thesis is that our present situation is more appropriately modeled on that of the disciples of Jesus. This is because sensitive Christians are now rightly alienated from our culture and institutions in a way that resembles the relation of the disciples of Jesus to the Jewish and Roman worlds.

To the eyes of the early Christians, the Jewish law, temple, and synagogues—as well as the Roman military and political powers— ceased to embody significant reality. They existed, and the Christians acknowledged this in many ways. These institutions continued to have the power to destroy and kill. But they lacked the power to give life. They belonged to a dying past. Analogously today, the received and actual structures of society appear already outdated. They have the power to crush opposition, but they are powerless to save either themselves or us. They exist out of inertia and blindness rather than to serve the ends the Christian seeks. The problem is not, as we once thought, only the failure of our institutions to fulfill the ideas to which they are ordered. Our new sense of limits shows us that many of these ideals misdirect our energies because they are unrealizable. For example, the planet cannot support all its inhabitants at the level of consumption of the industrialized nations; the ideal of high school education for all is beyond the economies of most countries; and the nuclear family turns out to collapse of its own weight when social pressure is removed. Further, even if the ideals were achievable, it now seems that they are not, after all, ideal. Progressive peoples in industrialized nations are not models for what all people should be. Even when society can afford education for all, compulsory education now appears to be humanly destructive. The nuclear family has oppressed women and damaged the emotional health of children. Our theory as well as our practice is now exposed as exploitative, racist, and sexist to the core.

We Christians have too often deplored alienation as an evil, failing to recognize the depth of alienation in the origins of our faith. We missed the point that all consciousness-raising tends to alienate, so that growth is, among other things, a process of alienation. We have not recognized that alienation is also liberation.

Still, our fear of the rapid rise of alienation in Western society was not ungrounded. Alienation can breed cynicism, and the liberation it affects can become license. By itself, alienation undercuts all meaning and produces nihilism, despair, and a purely destructive rage. The alienation we see among Jesus' disciples was not like this. They were grasped by a vision of a new and very different world that generated assurance, excitement, and commitment. An analogous vision appropriate to our time is already present in fragmentary ways, but it lacks the articulation that could transform it into a source of hope and a principle of action.

One reason for the continuing weakness of the urgently needed experience of the coming Kingdom is that our dominant theologies do not encourage such images. The dominant theologies of hope speak either of a structure of time appropriate to Christians in all historical epochs or of a final consummation of history. The liberation theologies point to fragments of the needed vision, but they are still predominantly committed to alienating us from our past forms and ideals. Our need now is a grasp of how the world of our children and grandchildren *might be* in contrast to how it will be if established patterns prevail.

Such a picture must be neither utopian nor realistic. A utopian picture pretends to a finality that belies the character of historical change. We can envision a much better future than the one that now seems probable, but even if it were realized, those who inhabit it will experience radical challenges and needs for continual change. A realistic picture assumes that only the patterns and principles of change discoverable in our recent past can be expected to function in the future. The realist thinks from what has been and is toward what can be, instead of confronting what is with what might be. The realist seeks immediate solutions to pressing problems without a holistic view of what would be involved in the concurrent solution of a complex matrix of problems. The realist's short-run propositions and counter-productive solutions of isolated problems cannot help us now.

It is extremely important to think globally of the future, but also extremely complex. Many of the clear mandates for the developed world and especially for our own country do not apply to the majority of the world's people. It would be pretentious at present for Americans to describe the hopeful future of China or of Chile. Our more pressing responsibility is to conceive a future for ourselves that is hopeful in global perspective. For us here and now, the church should be the vanguard of that future.

Some of the principles that must govern that future are now clear. First, there are the economic mandates. We should greatly reduce our consumption of the world's resources. Reduced consumption must be sought by changing, but not lowering, the quality of life. Overall reduction in consumption needs to be accompanied by substantial improvement in the economic condition of the poorest twenty percent of the population. And all who desire to be gainfully employed must have the opportunity to work.

Second, there are humanistic mandates. We must establish societies in which personal freedom to be different is compatible with a secure place in a supportive community. Differences of sex and race must not be linked with unequal access to opportunities desired by members of either sex or any race. Participation in establishing the structures and rules for community life must be maximized.

To list such mandates is a very different matter from providing a hopeful image of the future. Indeed, considering in this way what we "must" do becomes itself an oppressive "law." Further, it sets goals that seem to be in mutual conflict, and the apparent impossibility of achieving them leads to despair.

Just for this reason, it is vitally important to show that a society fulfilling these mandates is a possibility, that the requisite vision of hope is not far to seek. Because, at present, so many people feel hard-pressed to gain or maintain a comfortable life, we think that any cuts in consumption must entail hardships. But this is not true. Our present economic system creates wants and needs faster than it satisfies them. It produces wants psychologically by producing and advertising goods we got along very well without, and by the manipulation of taste and fashion. It produces needs by manufacturing products for short-term use and organizing communities physically in such a way that we are dependent on expensive transportation to get food, necessary services, and employment. Thus, in many parts of the non-industrialized world, a family can live very comfortably at a level of consumption that would be miserable or impossible in New York or Los Angeles. We must not suppose that human beings are condemned to crave unneeded goods or that society cannot organize itself so that less consumption is needed for a decent life.

The coming age must be radically alienated from the view that, beyond a level of modest comfort, the quality of life is correlated with the quantity of possession or consumption. On the contrary, status must be associated with skill in achieving the most with the least energy and goods. The value of persons will not be correlated to their production but to the quality of their personal lives and their contributions to the lives of others. Hence, competition for goods, while it will not cease, will occur without social approval. Economic incentives can still be applied as necessary to ensure that needed productive work is done, but the purpose of life will not be bound up with production. Finding useful work for all who need it will take precedence over maximum efficiency of production or profits. To employ persons usefully and healthfully, to reduce the consumption of energy, and to produce more nutritious food, agricultural production would be de-industrialized and become again more labor-intensive.

Cities should be progressively reconstructed in such a way that stores, services, and places of work are all readily accessible to dwellings without private cars or expensive systems of public transportation. Buildings should be constructed to take maximum advantage of sun and local weather conditions, and solar energy should rapidly supplant fossil fuels and nuclear energy as the primary source. Paolo Soleri's arcologies show how this can be accomplished as soon as we are prepared to direct our resources to these ends. His cities would free vast areas now covered by suburban sprawl for agricultural production.

Soleri's arcologies would encourage new lifestyles and new forms of community. They would combine privacy with ready access to public places, and they would facilitate increased participation in community affairs. They would make possible the needed combination of individual freedom and communal support.

To live now from the vision of such a future disengages us from the day-by-day decisions of present political and economic life. This can be dangerous. Much of the counter-culture of the sixties was ineffective and self-destructive because of its disengagement from the dominant culture. Primitive Christianity is often faulted for its failure to work at reforming the Roman Empire. But there may be times when withdrawal of psychic energy from much of the contemporary scene may be healthy and creative, and today may be such a time.

Specifically, what has the church to say today with respect to the great political issues? Should we keep taxes high to slow inflation in spite of the probable increase of unemployment, or should we lower taxes to reduce unemployment in spite of the probable acceleration of inflation? Is that the issue on which we have a word from the Lord? I think not. The whole debate goes on in the context of trying to shore up the present economic system and increase the gross national product. The absurdity stems from the fact that the goal of all parties to the debate is probably impossible and is certainly immoral. We must hope they all fail, so that fundamentally different approaches to our problems, now outside the arena of political discussion, will be considered. The church will do better to invest itself in these other approaches rather than to bind itself more tightly to dying institutions.

This may appear to be brutally indifferent to the real suffering of real Americans, whereas indifference is never a possibility for the church. But the question is not concern but strategy. Will we contribute more to relief or suffering by relying on the outdated methods now so fully established or by experimenting with others that are appropriate to a hopeful future? I believe we do better to live from the hopeful future rather than to involve ourselves more deeply in issues as now posed. Meanwhile, we can make our proposals to the government, just in case someone might listen.

If the nation were prepared to think from a hopeful future instead of "realistically," new policies could be quickly developed. Instead of encouraging Americans to buy cars and suburban homes so as to employ workers to produce goods that damage us all, the same money would employ workers to build experimental cities designed to use far less energy in the future. As the city was built, the workers could themselves live there and could then require fewer goods for comfortable living. They could work fewer hours so that more persons could be employed. Meanwhile, agricultural policies could be reversed so as to encourage simple family or communal farms and reduce the grip of agro-business in food production. Labor could gradually replace expensive equipment and high energy consumption.

Although there are, thus, policy changes in government that are suited to the new age, the most important role remains especially appropriate for the church—that is, the role of embodying its norm. The new age calls for quite different bases for making decisions than those by which we have been governed in the recent past. Money is a useful tool for accomplishing worthwhile ends but is not a measure of success or worth. Finding ways together to bring a viable society into being takes precedence over attainment of status in the existing society. The church has given at least lip service to such principles throughout its history; therefore, far more readily than the government, it can become the teacher of the new age. But it can teach effectively only if within itself it bodies the new age forth in advance.

I have presented an image of the church and suggested some concrete implications of that image. You may disagree with the specifics, but if you will spell out for yourself the meaning of being the vanguard of the new age, I doubt that you will find the implications for liberals and conservatives alike less radical than I do. We are called to bold new ventures of faith.

If we view the actuality of the American church in the mid-seventies in light of this image, we may be tempted to say it is not truly an image of the church at all, but only a utopian vision or idealistic fantasy. Even if there are grounds for such an image in Christian origins, one may argue, there are none in the present reality. This is a serious challenge to the image; for though the image does not intend to be a description, it can function as an image only if there are grounds for it in the given actuality—only if it is an accentuation of a tendency already present—only if church members can recognize something about themselves in it and be persuaded through it to think in new ways about their corporate life. Hence, it is important to my case to argue not that the church as a whole is now effectively functioning as the vanguard of the new age, but that its present life contains a tendency in this direction that can, in our unique historical period, gain a much greater prominence and effect. I shall clarify my claim around six points.

1. *Like all the institutions of our society, the church functions primarily to sanction and sustain received structures and norms.* More explicitly than others, it casts a "sacred canopy" over what is currently approved. Nevertheless, unlike other institutions, the church subscribes to principles that constantly bring into question both its own practices and those of other institutions.

2. *Most Christian theology, when it does not simply share in sanctioning the current situation, criticizes it in light of the longer tradition.* It looks to the past to illumine the present, and it tries to show that much of this past is *still* viable. It adjusts the tradition as little as is necessary to take account of what is inescapable in the advance of knowledge and the change of culture. Thus, it hardly appears as the vanguard of

the new age. Nevertheless, it continues to affirm a faith that has always looked to a new future rather than to a restoration of the past. At its best, it takes this openness to the future seriously, thematizes it, and even itself becomes open.

3. *Christian ethics for the most part, when it goes beyond expressing the prejudices of the speaker, does so by appeal to supposed Christian principles.* These are applied to changing conditions, and conclusions are drawn. Both in the sphere of personal morality and in that of social policy, Christian ethics, despite disclaimers, is usually legalistic. Protests against legalism, such as situation ethics, too easily replace intelligent reflection with unchecked spontaneity of response. But there are those who recognize that antinomianism is no more Christian than is legalism, that the Christian's vocation is to take bearings in the present from the age to come, and that to see what is in the light of what may be is to see it rightly. Christians are free from the law because they live by the norms of what is not yet.

4. *The official pronouncements of the church reflect the legalism of its dominant ethics.* The church typically addresses problems only as they capture attention through the daily paper and telecasts. It then takes its position with respect to issues on the basis of vaguely Christian humanistic values and a generalized goodwill. More conservative churches make more explicit the appeal to traditional Christian teaching or even offer proof-texts, but they do so only by turning the gospel into law in a more rigid way than even liberal ethicists. Still, church leadership is on the whole more open than most of "the establishment" to adapt thought and practice to new perspectives as they arise.

5. *It is sometimes commented that the church adopts organizational patterns and managerial methods only as these are discredited in industry.* Be that as it may, few could judge that the present cultures of the church are a vanguard of the age to come. My own denomination operates with a tightly closed shop system for the ministry. In a time when it is apparent that we need to share the work more widely if we are to welcome women who are entering ministry, we retain an all-or-nothing principle—either full-time work or no ministerial status. Yet, I suspect that under pressure from those who will benefit by structures more appropriate to the new age, the church will bend and adapt more extensively than most other institutions.

6. *Most local churches are maintenance operations.* They have no serious intention of evangelizing their communities or even their own members. They have no goals for themselves beyond gradually changing types of programs to hold the interest and loyalty of their

members and to replace them as they leave or die. Their music, rhetoric, and lifestyle often feel more like enclaves from the past than vanguards of the future. However, these communicate to sensitive members a restiveness about the present world that makes them peculiarly sensitive to visions of the new.

Hence, the church, despite its all-too-human frailty, has the potential to be the vanguard of the new age. It has this potential because, despite its immersion in the culture, it is partially independent of the culture. Now one might say that any group that maintains its own distinctive heritage of culture is indeed partly analogous to that of ethnic or cultural minority groups. Yet, there is a significant difference. The ethnic minorities have two choices: Either they conserve their heritage and thereby maintain their differences, or else they assimilate to the dominant culture. Much of church life also moves between these two poles. But the church has a third possibility: It can critically objectify both its traditions and the dominant culture and respond to creative new possibilities. Thus, the church can be the vanguard of the new age, whereas other subcultures in our society, though they may contribute to the new age, are not appropriately imaged as its vanguard.

II

When we ask why the church has the ability to objectify both itself and the dominant culture, we are brought to my second image. The church is *the focus of the presence of Christ*. To the extent that Christ is present in the church, the church can be the vanguard of the new age.

This is either a bold claim or a matter of definition. I intend it partly as each. It is, in the first place, a definition, because I mean by "Christ" that which moves us beyond what we have been, creatively transforms us, and opens us to the future. But it is also a bold claim, because I affirm that (1) what thus moves us is the incarnate presence of the transcendent divine Word of Logos, (2) the Logos is particularly present in the church, and (3) its effective presence in the church is due both to the words of Jesus and to a field of force deriving from him. I will offer a brief explanation of these three claims.

1. The church fathers followed the prologue to John's Gospel in understanding the Logos not simply as human words or as analogous words spoken by God, but as the creative principle of cosmic order and meaning. Unfortunately, there was a tendency to associate this principle with immutable laws of nature and morality in some tension with the biblical sense of historical change and movement toward the promised future. Hence, in the end, the notion of Logos,

introduced into the Trinity to counterbalance the immutability and impassibility of the Father and to account for the divine acts of creation and incarnation, was assimilated to the notion of the Father and failed in its purpose. But this was because the Greeks thought of the cosmos as eternal and its principles as unchanging. Today, we can speak of the history of nature from the big bang to the present, and we see the laws of nature too as evolving. The Logos is not a set of primordially established laws, but that structuring of possibility by virtue of which ordered novelty and novel order appear in the world. The Logos does not impose laws on the world but offers itself to the world for the world's realization. Insofar as it is embodied, the world is creatively transformed toward what it can become. The embodiment of the Logos is Christ. By virtue of Christ, the future need not be the mere result of the past. To whatever extent Christ is present, we live from Christ's future.

2. The Logos is everlastingly present everywhere, but its presence is differentiated in two ways. First, as already indicated, it presents itself in terms of ever-changing possibilities. Second, its presence varies from triviality to overwhelming importance. My claim is that the church, by naming the Logos Christ, encourages openness to it and thereby allows it to be more effective.

To see this, consider the consequences of denying the reality of the Logos. It is quite possible to suppose that the events of the past rule, without remainder, the present and the future. This results when the scientific effort to explain the present as effect in terms of the past as cause becomes the model for general thought. But even before the rise of science, most people felt themselves to live in a closed universe. For the higher religions, the goal usually has been to accept necessity, to return to the original unity, or to gain release from the meaningless flux of events. Perhaps few are ever fully consistent in their denial of novelty, but the sense of closure has dominated much of the sensibility of humankind. Where the Logos is recognized, it is in terms of law and order. For example, in the Enlightenment it was called natural law and conscience. These names directed attention to it, but instead of encouraging openness to its gift, they elicited efforts to obey established rules.

It was in Israel that people turned from the past and from the sense of eternal order to the recognition that God offered a new future. This future was pictured as the Day of the Lord and the Resurrection of the Dead. These expectations meant that one could live toward a future unlike anything that had occurred, a future given by God and not produced by the past. In that future, the righteousness of God would be vindicated. Still, for human beings this was a prospect of judgment that could not be altogether relished.

In Christian imagery, that judgment was completed in the cross of Christ. The future toward which we move is now grace rather than judgment. However we demythologize our images, it remains that to recognize as Christ the power that draws us into a new future is to trust it and welcome it, even when it uproots us from past habits and destroys past prejudices. Faith in Christ must involve basic trust in the giver and sustainer of life. Further, when it is recognized that Christ is the incarnation of the Logos, faith in Christ cannot be a basis for narrowness of vision and exclusion of unwelcome truth.

Of course, the church has distorted its message in all sorts of ways. The doctrine of election becomes a divine determinism that closes the future as effectively as fatalism or materialism. The future is presented as terrifying judgment instead of grace; Christ is identified with blind repetition of past legalism. Nevertheless, in its scripture and liturgy, the church names the Logos as Christ and understands that Christ is the Logos. Hence, it is in the church that Christ is most effectively present.

3. Christ is present in the church not only as the everlasting Logos but also as Jesus. There are not two opposing forms of presence; for the Logos opens us to Jesus, and Jesus opens us to the Logos. Jesus opens us to the Logos both by his words and by a field of force derived from him.

We are opened to the Logos by Jesus' teaching in two ways. We have already noted that trust is important; and Jesus' teaching of God's profligate love, as well as his words of assurance, inspires trust. But we are opened to the Logos also when our established security is shattered. As long as we believe that our wisdom and our virtue basically suffice, we are loathe to let go of our achievements. But such letting go is required if we are to be transformed by the Logos. When we hear Jesus' words, our nakedness is made evident to us, our defenses are broken down. We are ready to accept as a gift what we cannot attain by our efforts. We are open to the Logos, and Christ can become real in us.

The power of Jesus' words was fully appreciated in the early church, but there was another and deeper tradition of Jesus' saving work that has been harder for the modern mind to grasp. It is most powerfully captured in Paul's phrase "in Christ." For Paul, to be a believer was to be in Christ. This is a real, objective condition into which one enters or is drawn, rather than only a subjective state one develops. In his article on *"en Christô"* in Kittel's *Dictionary of the New*

Testament, Walter Grundmann suggests that we can think of this as a field of force generated by the life and passion of Jesus. Jesus is present as an effective power throughout this field of force. To enter the field is to be conformed in some measure to him.

In the first centuries, there was no doubt but that the church was identical with this field of force. It was renewed as Jesus was re-presented in the eucharist. It was experienced as life-transforming power. To know Jesus' presence in this field of force, to be conformed to him, was also to share in his openness to God's future and hence to the Logos. The presence of Christ as Jesus and of Christ as Logos were united.*

It is harder for us today to appropriate this powerful sense of Jesus' presence in the church. Our life in the church is all too continuous with our experience of the world in general. Our doctrines of the church and our explanations of the eucharist have become progressively more subjective. We have no categories for thinking of the effective presence of the past except memory, and in memory we suppose that all the agency lies in the remembering. But our liturgy and piety still attest to a presence of Jesus that is not exhausted in our theories. If we can find convincing ways to articulate it again, the experience will grow clearer, and the church will become more authentically the body of Christ. As the field of force of the crucified Jesus takes on new strength, the lives of Christians will be more fully conformed to him and the church will be in fact what it is in potency.

III

Of the two images I have proposed, one is in the prophetic tradition, the other, in the priestly. In the past generation, the prophetic tradition has been interpreted chiefly in political terms and the priestly in individualistic ones. We have contrasted social witness and personal conversion and piety. Yet, we all know that this is a false dichotomy. There is no effective social witness apart from deep, life-controlling, Christian conviction, and there is no genuinely Christian piety that ignores the needs of the world.

I have proposed an image in the prophetic tradition that is not primarily political in the usual sense. I have proposed an image in the priestly tradition that is more objective and communal than those that have dominated the recent past. My conviction is that not only are the two images, and the traditions they represent, mutually supportive,

---

*This section is a summary of major parts of the Christology developed in *Christ in a Pluralistc Age*. Westminster, 1975.

but that in their depths they are identical. The community that lives as the vanguard of the new age is the community that lives in and from the presence of Christ. The community that lives in and from the presence of Christ cannot be other than the vanguard of the new age. Our need is not to persuade social activists to become personally devout or the individually pious to express their concern for others intelligently and relevantly. Our need is to clarify what truly effective Christian action and truly Christian piety are in our time; for one cannot live from the Kingdom apart from Christ nor from Christ apart from the Kingdom.

8

The Holy Spirit and Leadership by Proposal

My reflections on leadership in the church fall under four headings. First, I will briefly comment on the general separation of theology from practice that afflicts our church life. Second, I will discuss the claim of process theology to help overcome this separation and how it understands God to be at work in the ordinary affairs of the world. Third, I will discuss the strengths and weaknesses of a theory of leadership offered by Rensis Likert as a norm for church leadership style, and, fourth, I will propose leadership by proposal as a way both of implementing Likert's intentions and adapting them to the particular needs of the church.

I

Discussion of church leadership styles shares with discussion of most other aspects of church practice a certain distance from theology. The distance results from developments on both sides. On the one side, theology has become a university discipline, clearly marked off from other departments of knowledge, itself fragmented, and breed-

Prepared for a conference on leadership styles held at Claremont in January 1982, and co-sponsored by the Center for Parish Development and the Center for Process Studies. In its original form, this paper was an appendix to a presentation by Ted Weeden on Likert 4 and the role of the Holy Spirit in Christian leadership.

121

ing its specialists. Its topics and approach rise not out of the present practice of the church but out of the history of the academic discipline.

On the other side, discussions of practice have sought their substance from disciplines developed to deal with other communities and institutions. If practice guided by these disciplines is in fact Christian, this is more by good fortune and remnants of Christian habits of mind than by conscious decision based on theologically informed reflection.

The problem is accentuated when the theological tradition to which appeal is made is that of a different culture with a different church life. In central Europe, from which we have imported our most scholarly theology, church life centers on catechesis and the proclamation of the word, the state plays a major role in the finances of the church, and much of church practice is settled by long-established European customs. A theology that enables the preacher to move from text to sermon often appears adequate.

But what is said in that theology cannot, without a great deal of reflection, serve American "pastoral directors" in the multiplicity of their functions. It does not clarify either pastoral counseling or church administration. When theologians accentuate the transcendence of God and argue that God's acts intersect the world only at "points," the virtual irrelevance of theology to church practice is assured. The "points" are almost impossible to identify in normal church life.

When theology makes itself irrelevant to decisions about the weekly life of the parish, those responsible for such decisions must, of course, turn elsewhere. Those responsible for pastoral counseling have turned to other mental health professions and the psychological theory by which their practice is shaped. Those responsible for administering the institutions of the church turn to management theory developed for other institutions.

The discipline of practical theology or pastoral theology has been asked to provide an alternative. But it has not been able to do so. Faculties are organized in terms of specializations. Theologians have primary responsibility for historical and systematic theology. Those who have the task of preparing ministers for their pastoral functions specialize in particular functions. There is much talk of building bridges between theology and reflection about ministerial functions, but once these disciplines are defined in their separateness, little is accomplished by "bridging."

Our need is not primarily for further development of departmental scholarship. It is instead for Christian reflection about real issues and problems. The Christian ethos has been effective, even when not consciously reflected upon, in influencing the development of pastoral counseling and church administration, to stay with the two examples that have been used above. But the risk constantly grows that as the ethos becomes weaker, the church will fail to make appropriate choices. Culturally dominant practices and habits of mind are in danger of being accepted uncritically. Today, to think as Christians requires that we learn to think *self-consciously* as Christians. In the broad sense of the term, that is theology, although it may not be the case that professional theologians can contribute any more than can others to the task.

<h1 style="text-align:center">II</h1>

One claim of process theology is that it deals more realistically and concretely with the way God works in the world and in the church. It resists departmentalization and takes as its task, at least in principle, the whole range of questions that Christians raise in our actual contemporary situation. These include questions of pastoral counseling and church administration. They include also the question of what style of leadership is most appropriate to the church. In dealing with such questions, process theologians find empirical data and historical information as pertinent as creedal formulations and traditional doctrines. But it is equally true that we find creedal formulations and traditional doctrines as pertinent as empirical data and historical information. What is important is to refuse to parcel out these materials among a set of disciplines which then treat them in separation from one another. What is thus pulled apart is no more likely than Humpty Dumpty to be put back together again.

The challenge of this conference to a "process theologian" is to make good on the implicit claim to be able to talk about practical matters theologically in a way that is really helpful. To be helpful could be either to provide theological justification for what the Center for Parish Development is currently doing or to suggest modifications that are commended by theological reflection. Unfortunately, I do not have the detailed familiarity with the Center's work to make a possible real engagement with it. However, Paul Dietterich shared with me a critique recently written to him by Dean M. Kelley of the National Council of Churches that expresses a theologically based dissatisfaction.

The central thesis of Kelley's critique is summarized in the following passage from his letter: "I thought the highly developed praxis you had shared with us was elaborately and oppresively *horizontal*. It assumed as given the purpose(s) of the church without devoting comparable skill and effort to helping the congregation determine those purposes of mission and ministry from sources *outside* itself and its environment, viz., from the Holy Spirit and the Scriptures."

Whether the criticism is accurate is for those who are closer to the Center's word to judge. That it is appropriate to most church practice seems to me evident. It makes three points with which a process theologian must agree. First, clarification of purpose is prior to improvement of methods of attaining the goal. Second, clarification of purpose (and, I would add, improvement of the procedure) cannot be separated from the present work of the Holy Spirit. Third, our reflection about purpose (and practice) should be grounded in scripture.

On the other hand, by associating these three sound points with the image of the "vertical," Kelley suggests a mode of thinking that dichotomizes in a way that does not appear to process theologians to be biblical. Apparently, for Kelley, questions of practice belong to one dimension—the horizontal—whereas questions of purpose belong to another dimension—the vertical. Presumably, theology deals only with the vertical dimension, whereas it is appropriate to turn to secular authorities for guidance in implementing the purposes there defined. This separation of means from ends is largely responsible for our present problems and is unlikely to help toward solution.

Consider what is meant by saying that our relation to scripture is vertical. In principle, this imagery de-historicizes scripture. Apparently, scripture does not come to us as the record of decisive past events and the embodiment of the thinking and testimony of the great figures who shaped Israel and Christianity. It comes to us instead from "above." The scholarly work of the past two centuries is set aside as essentially irrelevant by such an image. All the problems that scholarship has helped us to overcome return.

Much the same must be said when the relationship to the Holy Spirit is declared to be vertical. The Holy Spirit cannot then be seen as the creative activity of God manifest in all life or the redemptive and freeing work of God in history and in human individuals. Creative and redemptive processes on a horizontal level will have to be described without reference to God. God's activity will have to be viewed as intervention into an otherwise non-divine process.

I do not know, of course, whether this is what Kelley intends or desires by the imagery of horizontal and vertical. But it is what that imagery has often meant in the past. It is a dualism against which process theology also has argued.

Thus far, I have done no more than to clarify the stance of process theology in a very general way. It opposes the dualism that separates the work of God from the biological, historical, sociological, and psychological processes that constitute our actual world. It opposes a view of these processes that does not take seriously into account scripture and the Holy Spirit and the primacy of purpose over method.

To reflect on leadership style in light of scripture brings sharply into focus the question of the charismatic element in leadership. In that regard, I want to offer insight into the work of the Holy Spirit in process perspective, and explore how that work can influence our thinking about leadership style. To do so, I will need to move to more general reflections about the role of God in the universal process.

If we try to think about the world in abstraction from God, our efforts to explain any particular event will ordinarily, and I think properly, seek to account for it in the antecedent circumstances out of which it arises. This is the method of all of the sciences. For most sciences, this leads to a methodological determinism. To understand why an event had the character it had, one seeks to learn what, in the situation in which it arose, determined it to have that character. Science is the quest for such determinations. The assumption of many scientists and of many whose thought patterns are influenced by science is that the scientific explanation will become more and more complete and that in principle it *could* be exhaustive. This assumption, at least implicitly, is that every event happens as it does because of antecedent circumstances. This is metaphysical determinism.

Against metaphysical determinism, it can be argued that an increasing portion of science deals with statistical probabilities instead of specific necessities. The mathematically exact predictions with respect to the objects of ordinary perceptions are subject to explanation in terms of statistical probabilities applicable to the very large number of component entities. The pressure of gas on a surface can be predicted with considerable exactness although it results from the activities of molecules that cannot be individually predicted with such exactness.

This complication of methodological and metaphysical determinism does not affect the general idea that each event is the product of antecedent events. It simply requires that an element of chance be acknowledged in reference to minute individuals. The world must now be accounted for by a combination of chance and necessity.

Western humanists have not been satisfied with this scientific or scientistic vision. They have insisted that when we deal with human beings, we must include purpose and freedom as explanatory factors. To do so they have insisted on separating human beings drastically from the rest of the world. Even so, they have had great difficulty showing how a historical event can be explained except as an outgrowth of the conditions in which it occurs. The entertainment of a purpose by a human being seems to call for essentially the same kind of explanation as anything else.

Yet, a great deal of our ordinary human language and experience seems to assume a different situation—one in which the present event really transcends its past. The transcendence in question is not a matter of chance versus necessity. Of course, much in an event of human experience is the necessary or inevitable outcome of the past, and perhaps some elements are random chance. But we also are aware of ourselves as choosing among alternatives that are not simply present in the past out of which we come. There are a variety of relevant possibilities, some better than others. Occasionally, we make choices in the light of careful analysis of such alternatives and anguished decision. But what is spread out in analytic detail in such times characterizes all human experience in a much less conscious way.

Apart from the effectiveness for us of relevant possibilities that stand beyond the realized actuality of the past, we *could* be nothing but the product of that past. Moral responsibility, personal freedom, and decision can occur only because we are confronted by such possibilities for our existence. But whence come these relevant possibilities? They cannot come from the world, for they transcend the world. They cannot come from ourselves, for they are required to constitute us as what we are and become. Process theologians name the source of these possibilities "God." We acknowledge in the most literal and straightforward sense that not only freedom but life itself is the continually renewed gift of God. God, as the one who enters into our very being or experience moment by moment to free and enliven us, is quite properly called the Holy Spirit.

It is important to see that the work of the Holy Spirit is in no way competitive with our own freedom and responsibility. It is not the case that the more historical events are explicable as the work of the Holy Spirit, the less place there is for human agency. Quite the contrary. Since the work of the Holy Spirit is to enliven us and make us free, the more effective is the Holy Spirit, the more we are effective as truly human agents. It is when the work of the Holy Spirit is blocked that we become slaves to the past and the true explanation of history is in terms of brute forces.

I have spoken of life and freedom as the work of the Holy Spirit. But there is a third element that is equally important. Freedom is not simply the possibility of doing many things. Freedom and responsibility arise in the context of evaluation. Some things are better to do than others. The same act of the Holy Spirit through which a space is opened up for our free decision is one that calls us to the best. The Holy Spirit enlightens, guides, directs, and lures. It makes thinking possible, but it embodies a wisdom and a truth that always exceed our rational powers.

This is one reason that the separation of ends and means is so inappropriate. We cannot by reason, or by submitting to the authority of scripture or Holy Spirit, establish a purpose that then remains fixed while we go about implementing it without further reference to scripture or Holy Spirit. That would be to return to the letter and the law. On the contrary, the working of the Spirit is pervasive and never to be captured in a final statement. Our task is to learn, individually and collectively, to be open to the Spirit, responsive to it, freed and enlivened by it, and thus constantly led in appropriate ways beyond our understanding. The role of leaders in the church is to facilitate the working of the Holy Spirit.

Process theology hopes that it can make some contribution to moving from this general theological claim to specific suggestions about leadership style. This is a task not unlike that faced by St. Paul. Paul found that he was misunderstood in two directions. Some rejoiced in what he said about freedom but interpreted it as a justification for license. They sought a freedom from the repression embodied in the law and thus a release to act on their private desires, whatever the effect on others. Paul taught that this was not real freedom but a new slavery. Others felt the need to structure their new Christian lives in terms of old and new rules and regulations. For them, Christian faith must express itself in specific forms of life. Paul saw this also as a new slavery. Our task, like that of Paul, is to develop a sufficiently clear notion of what true freedom is and of how it grows so that we may serve the Holy Spirit and not some other. The alternatives of antinomianism and legalism are as pervasive in our society as they were in Paul's. To whatever extent we succeed, we will be able to say that appropriate leadership is that which sets people free in the authentic and Christian sense of "free."

The reference to Paul points to our primary dependence upon the scripture for our task. We must learn to use the scripture in the service of the Holy Spirit whose liberating work we can understand only through continual dependence upon scripture. The pages that follow are intended to illustrate the types of reflection about leadership style that develop within these parameters.

III

Likert 4 designates a leadership style that emphasizes participatory involvement in decision making among leaders and followers, at the opposite end of the scale from Likert 1, which is characterized by hierarchical authoritarianism. Although it is appealing because of its emphasis on shared human responsibility and human equality, Likert 4 is decidedly different from biblical models of leadership as these have been institutionalized in the church. Since Likert 4 clearly embodies many Christian norms, this could lead us to think that biblical and traditional leadership styles in the church are simply inferior. But I do not move in this direction. Likert 4 is important, but there are crucial ways in which it does not take account of particular leadership needs in the church.

In process perspective, we can speak of Christianity as the whole historical movement that has followed from the life, death, and resurrection of Jesus and the apostolic witness thereto. Today, much of this Christianity does not know itself as such. For example, many people who do not associate themselves consciously and intention- ally with Christianity live by democratic ideals whose historical origins depend upon the influence of the Christ event.

Within the whole Christian movement there are the churches. These are so structured as to bear witness to the initiating events and to keep alive the memory of their history. They may or may not embody the norms generated by the Christ event better than other communities or movements. But their intentional witness to Christ distinguishes them from other expressions of Christian influence. Of course, normatively the church responds to current needs out of its past and especially out of the Christ event.

Likert 4 is a generally good description of Christian ideals applied to management. But it does not show how the memory of the past is kept alive and effective, whereas this has been the primary and necessary preoccupation of the churches in their establishment of criteria for professional ministerial leadership. Likert 4 is certainly more Christian than Likert 1, 2, and 3, which represent variations in degrees of a leader's imposition of authority. Compared with them, Likert 4 is most likely to enliven and liberate and thus serve the Holy Spirit. But Likert does not deal with the specific requirement for leadership in the church. The church requires leaders who have been enculturated into the memory of the church, especially through study of the Bible, and who have learned to think about current issues out of that history. Specifically, the major objective requirement for leadership is a seminary education.

Leadership styles among a group of people all of whom are equally informed by the memory of the Christian movement can follow Likert 4. But where many in a church are but little shaped by this memory and are formed instead by other histories, Likert 4 provides no assurance that the identity and distinctive mission of the church will survive. Survival depends on the effective influence of the Christian memory in shaping the ongoing life of the church, and that requires weighting authority toward those who are most informed by this memory. In other words, it is normally appropriate that the community look for direction to those within it who have had the benefit of education designed to steep them in this memory. Nevertheless, these persons are or should be those who best know the importance of those values that are realized in Likert 4!

The problem posed for the church is, therefore, how those steeped in the church's memory can lead in such a way as to facilitate general participation in decision making while ensuring that this decision making will be deeply informed by the church's memory. This is no easy matter. It clearly means that Likert 1–3 are not to be adopted as normative models. But there must be an additional leadership role that is not expressed in Likert 4.

If the divine truth is understood to be exhaustively contained in a past that only the teacher adequately knows, then there seems to be no way to avoid authoritarian leadership. Those who know the divine truth must give direction to the church. Those who do not know must follow. This idea is too easily associated with thinking of the relevation to scripture as vertical versus horizontal, but the view of the church as living out of its memory need not have that kind of consequence.

If we assume that those who share in the present life of the church have some implicit commitment to being informed by the church's history, then the role of those who are best informed about that history could be simply the providing of relevant information. Likert 4 would not require much modification if this model were adopted. Once the relevant information was provided, it could be supposed, the group would then proceed to arrive at decisions in a fully egalitarian way.

However, there is a difference between having information about the past—for example, the Bible—and being informed by it in one's perceptions of the present world. If one's basic perceptions are but little affected by the history that produced the Bible and has continued to form the church since then, relevant items of information about that history will be assimilated into a quite different perspective. The identity and authentic continuity of the church will not be assured. Those who are steeped in the tradition and formed by its historical memories perceive new issues in a way that cannot be exchanged for bits of information.

I am rejecting the role of the leader as decider for the group, and the role of the leader as simply providing information for the group to dispose of. What is the alternative? I suggest that the task of leadership is to sustain awareness of the tension between the horizon within which most members of the group, perhaps including the leader, normally make decisions, and the horizon that is shaped by the church's memory. The goal is to reduce the tension by widening our moral horizons in the direction of the Christian horizons. This is one major function of corporate worship.

Consider an example. The topic of peace is one that many churches are now urging as of pressing importance. It is obviously bound up with national and international policies. Most of us have very strong identification with our nation and its interests. Most of the time, we view events in China, Iran, or Central America in terms of how they support or weaken the position of the United States. This is hardly less true of a typical group of church members than of others.

Nevertheless, many persons who do habitually read the newspaper and support political policies within this horizon recognize that there is, or may be, some tension between these habits and what is called for by the Christian gospel. That it has a universalistic character is widely acknowledged, and those who are designated as leaders are expected by others to view matters more from this wider perspective and to bring this wider perspective to bear upon issues. This is a healthy expectation that a Christian leader should not belittle. But, of course, no Christian should be content to allow the national perspective to remain unchallenged in her or his own life. So the expectation of the leader is not only representation of the Christian perspective but help in Christianizing the perspectives of all. Corporate worship, including the sermon, and teaching are among the ways in which this leadership function is exercised.

But how does this differ from the authoritarian approach? It differs in several ways. First, although a theological education will on the whole do more to ground one in the Christian tradition than other modes of formation in the modern world, the difference is one of degree. The pastor by no means has a monopoly on Christian memory. The church needs structures through which to check the pastor's claims against the corporate memory of the congregation and the wider church. On the whole, a system of checks and balances here is better than vesting final authority in any one place.

Second, the concrete issues faced by a congregation are not settled by the perspective in which they are approached. Many other types of knowledge and understanding need to be brought to bear, with respect to most of which the pastor is less informed than other members of the community.

Third, the Christian perspective is itself a constantly changing one. It changes by assimilation of elements from other sources. For example, the Christian perspective today on sexuality is quite different from the Christian perspective on this subject in the early nineteenth century. We must credit Freud with an immense contribution to the reshaping of our perspective. In more modest ways, the perspectives brought by all members of the Christian community have something to contribute to the perspective itself. The one who is educationally immersed in the Christian tradition cannot singlehandedly judge the worth of other perspectives for the shaping of the emerging Christian perspective.

IV

The implications of all this for me are that the role of the leader designated by the church is one of *proposing* rather than pronouncing, informing, or simply facilitating the interaction of the other members of the community. In respect to issues dealing with world peace, for example, the role of the leader is to propose church policies and actions that seem to her or to him to arise out of the Christian perspective. Of course, other Christians are encouraged to do so also, but there is some likelihood that those who have given special attention to immersing themselves in the Christian perspective may be able to offer better-informed proposals. Such proposals will set the state in a way that is likely to lead to a different type of discussion than would proposals emanating from the Pentagon or from one or our major national parties. But the proposal is for the purpose of eliciting reflection and discussion rather than determining the outcome. The appropriate action for the church to take cannot be settled apart from the wisdom that is shaped by many forms of life experience other than that of professional leaders. The process of arriving at a decision on the basis of which the church can involve itself effectively in action will be more like Likert 4 than like anything else on the Likert scale.

What I mean by a proposal is what Whitehead called a proposition. A proposition is a way the world, or some feature of the world, may be. Some propositions are true in the sense that the world, or some feature of the world, already is the way the proposition holds it to be. But it is more important that a proposition be interesting than that it be true. The only proposals worth making are interesting ones. An interesting proposal presents a possibility that is likely to be in some tension with the way things are, or, at least, with the way things are ordinarily perceived to be. To whatever extent the proposal interests the hearers, the hearers are changed—that is, hearers perceive the world differently. To continue with the example, the hearers may perceive the effects of U.S. policy from the point of view of people in China, Iran, or Central America instead of only from their own point of view. Once this other point of view is taken, even fragmentarily and fleetingly, one cannot return entirely to the mode of perception that dominated before. The resultant discussion must be different to some extent from the one that would have taken place had this not happened.

Hence, the leader's role as proposer is not merely one of suggesting ideas already quite familiar to others as topics for discussion. Significant proposals inherently alter the context of discussion. A pastor who is incapable of making such proposals cannot be an effective leader and may have to resort to authoritarian styles. A pastor capable of such proposals is, in fact, drawing the community into the Christian vision and thus reducing the tension between ordinary and Christian perspectives.

In conclusion, this more practically oriented discussion should be related to the more theological discussion that preceded it. In that discussion, I opposed the separation of means and ends correlated with a distinction of the horizontal and the vertical. I affirmed the priority of purpose over technique and the importance of the authority of scripture and Holy Spirit. I argued that the Holy Spirit is God constitutively present in our experience, enlivening us, freeing us, and directing us through a call to transcend what we have been in a quite particular way. Leaders in the church should serve the Holy Spirit by facilitating this enlivening, freeing, and directing work. But this will be misunderstood and misperceived except as the church's memory, and especially scripture, are brought effectively to bear.

I have now argued that, for practical purposes, this means that the church rightly prepares leaders through an educational immersion in the church's history and a context in which practical issues are considered in light of that memory. However poorly seminaries perform their task, three or four years spent in the seminary context do encourage such immersion. The church must then give to those who have been so prepared sufficient authority that they can lead effectively. But this leadership must be service of the Holy Spirit. That means it cannot be authoritarian.

My proposal is that Christian leadership is normatively the leadership of proposal. A proposal enhances the freedom of the one to whom it is made. That which previously was not present in the horizon of meanings becomes through the proposal a likely possibility. The proposal elicits thought as well as decision. The hearer is encouraged to relate the new proposal to old ideas and expectations. The result can be creative imagination and conceptualization. Such creative activity is the enhancement of life.

There is, of course, no guarantee that those who hear proposals will be freed and enlived by them. Other responses are possible. What happens depends on the hearer. This is true of the proposals by which the Holy Spirit works in us as well. But to lead by proposals that are rooted in scripture and tradition is to work with the Holy Spirit. That appears to be an appropriate style of leadership for the church.

Part
III

An
Ecology
of the
Spirit

9

Wholeness Centered in Spirit

In recent reflections about the ideal for human existence, the language of wholeness and the language of spirit rarely go together. They connote quite different ideals in considerable tension with each other. To formulate the ideal of wholeness centering in spirit is to introduce the tension into the ideal itself. This provokes fresh reflection on the meanings of the key terms and on the nature of the human ideal.

This paper is written from the perspective of a Christian theologian. Theologians have spoken more of "spirit" than of "wholeness." Indeed, the heroes of the Christian tradition are not noted for their "wholeness." Yet, "wholeness" belongs to a family of words, including holiness, that have played a very prominent role in Christian history. And Christians who have largely lost the ability to think in terms of holiness have found the new ideas of holiness as wholeness, coming from humanistic psychology, appealing, if also somehow troubling.

The terms "spirit" and "wholeness" are both fluid in their meaning and use. In theology, also, there are diverse uses of these terms. There would be no difficulty in so defining them that the tensions

Reprinted by permission from *Spirit Centered Wholeness*, edited by H. Newton Malony, Michele Pape-Daniels, and Howard Clinebell. The Edwin Mellen Press, 1988. The essay was originally presented at a conference on this subject sponsored by the Institute for Religion and Wholeness in 1983.

they introduce would vanish, but little would be gained by such a procedure. I propose instead to present brief pictures of two human ideals. I associate one with wholeness, the other with spirit. Although I do not assert that others must have the same ideals in mind when they use these terms, I hope my use will not seem eccentric. It will be clear from these accounts that wholeness and spirit in these senses cannot be simply merged. That will pose the question as to whether there is another kind of wholeness that can center in spirit. I will argue that there is, and will offer a brief account of spirit-centered wholeness.

What will thereby be depicted, however, remains unsatisfactory. This spirit-centered wholeness lacks the attractive spontaneity and presence of the wholeness that is indifferent to spirit. The final proposal of the paper is that for the renewal of spontaneity without loss of spirit, we must move from spirit-centered wholeness to Spirit-centered wholeness.

The Ethical Ideal and the Ideal of Wholeness

There are many ideas of what human existence ideally should be. One of the most prominent, one that has seemed self-evident to many, is that of ethical righteousness. It seems that people *should* do in every instance what they should do. The problem of defining the ideal, then, is the problem of identifying the norms, rules, principles, or virtues by which this obligation is determined. The problem of realizing the ideal is the problem of overcoming inward resistance to the requirements of these norms.

Those who advocate the ideals connoted by wholeness and by spirit reject this ethical one as too limited. They do not, of course, propose that violation of ethical norms is desirable. But they believe that the life that centers in the effort to be righteous is inadequate and unsatisfactory.

The most thorough and influential theological discussion of the alternative ideals for human existence has been that of Søren Kierkegaard. He distinguished the aesthetic, the ethical, and the religious as the three great options. He identified them as stages, with a clear sense that the movement of progress was from the aesthetic to the ethical and from the ethical to the religious. If the Christian imposes this scheme on the alternatives now before us, the quest for wholeness will seem to be at the aesthetic stage, and the ideal of spirit at the religious. We could then suppose that the two alternatives to ethical righteousness are sub-ethical on the one side and supra-ethical on the other.

Such an analysis is not irrelevant to the contemporary scene. Some of the same psychological developments that have led to the ideal of wholeness have led also to the glorification of what Kierkegaard described as aesthetic. But those who seek wholeness are aware of the inadequacy of this sub-ethical response. They seek a mode of existence that will incorporate what is necessary and desirable in ethical conduct in a wider context. In that context, what truly conforms to ethical righteousness will be done as an expression of what one is rather than in opposition to one's continuing desires. This sets aside attention to rules and principles, but it encourages relationships with others, which will attain the ends sought by conformity to such rules and principles more effectively than does the preoccupation with ethical righteousness. In these ways, it resembles Kierkegaard's religious stage more than the aesthetic. It may be better understood as an alternative form of the religious than as a falling back to the aesthetic.

What is this alternative to the ideal of ethical righteousness that can be named as "wholeness"? It is, first, a rejection of dualism. The life lived according to the ethical ideal is inevitably dualistic. One tries to do what is right even when one does not want to do it. One experiences resistance to the right within oneself. In terms of the ethical ideal, the sources of this resistance are necessarily viewed as evil. One *ought* to be faithful to one's spouse. One desires another. That desire is evil, and when one acts upon it, that is a sin. The will to overcome that desire and to act righteously is good.

There is today a great deal of psychological wisdom pointing to the negative consequences of this dualism. The desire labeled evil does not go away, and the moral struggle against it leads to a preoccupation with illicit sexuality. There is a strong tendency to envy those who actually, or in the fantasy of the righteous, give way to temptation, and to desire their punishment because of this envy. There is also a strong tendency to blame others for the power of evil within oneself—witness the extensive blaming of women for the sins of men. If, on the other hand, one yields to temptation, this is followed or accompanied by intense feelings of guilt, which may not prevent repetition of the sin but which do have destructive consequences for the personality as a whole. These complex dynamics are today well known and do not require elaboration here.

The ideal to which I am pointing by "wholeness" rejects this dualism of right and wrong, good and evil, will and desire. It accepts human reality as it is with all of its wants and desires. It condemns nothing. It affirms that precisely when nothing is condemned, nothing becomes destructive. All one's impulses can be acknowledged and accepted for what they are. They should not be viewed hierarchically as if some were more noble than others. Each is what it is and has its rightful place in the whole. Sexuality is to be accepted and enjoyed as a pervasive aspect of life without any compulsive need for its genital expression but equally without guilt about that expression. In general, a mark of wholeness is freedom from compulsiveness and legalistic guilt.

What I am calling human wholeness in its ideal form is not found apart from relationships. Indeed, it is experienced and lived only in relationships. Because those who are whole persons accept the whole range of emotions within themselves, they can be themselves with others and allow others to be themselves as well. This does not make for trouble-free relationships. But it makes for authenticity, depth, genuine sharing, spontaneity, and growth. Whole persons can sustain long-term relationships, but they can also accept their rupture.

Those who are whole can enjoy others, but they have no need for the constant company of others. They do not need the admiration or affection of others as a basis for acceptance of themselves. Hence, they have no general need to please others or to win success or fame. They enjoy relationships with the world of nonhuman creatures as well as with human beings, and they can enjoy times of being alone with their own thoughts and feelings. They can enjoy beauty, but they have no compulsion to attain refined aesthetic tastes. They can enjoy being creative, but they have no need to demonstrate their gifts to themselves or to others. They are adventurous and curious, but they do not need to pile novelty upon novelty to avoid boredom.

Perhaps the central image for "whole" persons is "at-homeness." They are "at-home" in their bodies, in their conscious and unconscious feelings and desires, in their human relationships, and in their total natural environment. They are "at-home" with who they are, and therefore they are comfortable being just that.

Because they are "at-home" in themselves, they are free from defensiveness toward others. Others experience their warmth—that is, their openness, their concern, and their affection. One is not the object of good deeds or just treatment from the whole person. One is the recipient of acceptance and understanding.

The Ideal of Spirit

The ideal associated with spirit is a quite different alternative to the limitations of ethical righteousness. The ethical person attempts to make each decision rightly. The spiritual person is captured by a vision of what is needful or desirable and is dedicated to its service or realization. What is to be done is ordered by the convictions that the vision expresses and the commitments that follow from it. The vision may take innumerable forms. For example, it may be of a people freed from oppression, or of a world in which peace is secure, or of a society in which the fulfillment of each conduces to the fulfillment of all. It may combine such elements as these in a larger whole.

Persons of spirit in this sense live from and for visions such as these. This means that their personal fulfillment is subordinated to wider purposes. There is no inherent value in self-sacrifice, but when the larger good can be realized only through actions that are personally costly, these actions, including the laying down of one's life, will be taken.

Personal morality will also be relativized. The need to be morally pure, characteristic of the ethical life, is set aside. This does not mean that conformity to generally accepted ethical principles will be lightly ignored. But for the realization of the larger purposes, one's self-image as a righteous person may have to be sacrificed.

Relationships with others are important for spiritual persons. But these are not ends in themselves simply to be enjoyed or to be valued as means to personal growth. Relationships subserve the cause. It is precisely in shared commitment to that which is beyond themselves and beyond the relationships that the relationships attain their full meaning and depth.

Our psychological culture encourages the suspicion that those who commit themselves to overriding causes do so out of an emotional need. For example, one's need to be approved by others and by oneself may lead to dramatic acts of sacrifice. There is no doubt that "causes" attract people who have such psychological needs, often unhealthy ones. But if it is true that no one is committed to work for world peace because world peace is truly important and desirable, more important and desirable than personal satisfactions and enjoyments, then the idea of spirit is an illusion. The assumption of this paper is that spirit is just as real as emotion. That does not mean that there could be people of spirit whose convictions and commitments are free of emotional comcomitants. Indeed, in the real world, I assume that there are destroying aspects in these emotional comcomitants in all cases. The ideal associated with spirit, however, is that these concomitants not distort, and such distortion is sufficiently a matter of degree that we can understand the ideal of its elimination.

Persons who are genuinely and purely committed to inclusive purposes tend to experience the many aspects of their own personal existence with a certain detachment. Their identify is bound up with the service of the cause. This does not make their bodily and emotional needs disappear. To some extent, these can be correlated with the service of the cause, but for the most part some tension remains between emotion and spirit.

According to this ideal, people of spirit will not view this tension in dualistic terms as coming from evil and expressing itself in sin. If they speak of evil and sin, as they may well do, it will be in terms of the great social forces that make for oppression and war. But they know that in the process of serving the cause, they must deal with those aspects of their own makeup that make claims on them discontinuous with that service. How they do that varies greatly. Gandhi's choice of celibacy and sexual sublimation is one example. Others may choose a mode of alternation in which periods of ascetic devotion to the cause are balanced by others in which bodily and emotional needs are cared for. As another possibility, we will discuss later the ideal of wholeness centering in spirit. What is common to all of these is a conscious and reflective decision as to how to deal with the various aspects of one's personal existence.

Spiritual persons have great power over others. The unification of their lives and energies around a cause attracts others to that cause and to them as leaders. Justifications for narrower foci of live and primary attention to personal interests are shattered by contact with spiritual people. They are not comfortable to be around. They force decisions that most people do not want to make. But they fascinate as well as repel, and their words have authority.

The ideal of persons of spirit is of persons who are free from the need to be approved or liked. If they desire success, it is because their success is conducive to that of the cause. If they desire fame, it is because visibility and reputation enable them to increase their contribution to the cause.

The Combination of Wholeness and Spirit

Among the many possible ideals for human existence, I have sketched two, which I have distinguished with the key words *wholeness* and *spirit*. They are presented, of course, as ideals, not as descriptions of actual people. Nevertheless, they are not remote and unrealizable ideals. There are persons who approximate to wholeness as described and there are others who approximate to wholeness as described and there are others who approximate to spirit. Although most of us are far from embodying either ideal, to subscribe to one or the other is likely to exercise considerable influence in our lives.

The suggestion of the topic of this conference is that many of us find attractiveness in both ideals and desire in some way to combine them. The fact that we are holding such a conference also indicates that such a combination is not a simple matter.

The problem appears most clearly when we begin with wholeness. It may seem that the need would be simply to expand wholeness to include more and more, in this case, spirit. But when approached from this side, we find a double meaning in "wholeness." One idea is that of inclusiveness, the other, that of completeness and self-containedness. These are in tension. The ideal of wholeness I have sketched is dominated by the latter. It is, of course, inclusive of a great deal, but it is not inclusive of everything. Specifically, it is not inclusive of spirit. If if attempts to include spirit, it loses its completeness and self-containedness. It would not be expanded by such inclusion, it would be radically altered.

This is because this ideal of wholeness is realized by the rejection of heteronomous requirements laid upon oneself from beyond the self. The rejection is primarily of ethical requirements, but it must include those of the spirit as well. The nonhierarchical appreciation of all aspects of human existence is incompatible with ordering them to a purpose that transcends personal existence. This does not mean that the attainment of this ideal of wholeness excludes contributing to good causes. It does not. But these contributions must be expressions of concerns that arise nonhierarchically alongside other concerns. They cannot be all-consuming.

If wholeness and spirit cannot be brought together by an expansion of wholeness, can they be united from the side of spirit? The difficulties on this side as well are enormous. If, as we are likely to agree, Gandhi is a great spiritual leader of our century and comes as close as anyone to embodying the ideal of spirit, we will also agree that he did not embody the ideal of wholeness. For the sake of India and the world, he not only repressed or sublimated his sexuality, he also abused his body with extreme fasting. His emotional life and personal relationships, including those with his children, also suffered from his commitment to Indian independence. In these respects, he is not untypical of spiritual leaders. For example, it is saddening to observe the cost to self and family paid by many of the leaders in the struggle against the Vietnam War. In many cultures, it has been held that the ideal of spirit cannot mix with family life. The ideal of a wholeness centering in spirit, therefore, is in sharp contrast with the dominant ideals associated with spirit and with their major approximations in history. Nevertheless, the remainder of this paper will deal with the ideal of spirit-centered wholeness. The intention is not that this ideal displace all existing ideals including those of wholeness and of spirit. At least at our present juncture, we need a plurality of ideals. But for those such as myself who cannot abandon the ideal of spirit, who see it indeed as particularly needed in a time when catastrophe threatens all, but who are distressed by its historical role of denial of personal wholeness, the ideal of spirit-centered wholeness has importance and even urgency.

The Possibility and Limitations of Spirit-Centered Wholeness

Characteristic of people of spirit is the critical objectification of the various aspects of their own being. They reflect about their sexuality and their human relationships, for example, in light of their convictions and commitments. This does not itself conduce to wholeness. On the contrary, the ordering of these aspects of their lives to purposes that are alien to them more generally leads to sacrifices or to unintegrated alternations. To order one's life to the liberation of a people from political oppression probably necessitates the rejection of wholeness.

This follows from the fact that although the vision that controls commitment and conviction is a very large one, it is not itself inclusive. Those devoted to the liberation of a particular people from a particular oppression usually know that there are other needs in the world as well. But these other needs do not often constitute an effective part of their vision. Hence, they order their whole lives to the limited goal. This cannot be integrative of all aspects of their personal being.

The situation is only a little improved if they do concern themselves with the political liberation of all oppressed people. This has the advantage of relativizing the needs of one people and therefore reducing the likelihood that the liberation of one group will be at the expense of others. But with respect to the dimensions of personal experience, little is changed. All will be ordered to political ends.

The situation is changed, however, if the vision that shapes convictions and commitments is of a whole world of whole people. In this vision, it is clear that freedom from war and political oppression cannot be separated from the wholeness of personal life and personal relationships. The ordering of all aspects of one's existence to this goal will ideally involve their positive inclusion in an integrated form. In practice, of course, compromises are required. For the sake of the wholeness of all, some may have to sacrifice their wholeness and even their lives. But in this vision, it is recognized that the failure to attain to personal wholeness is a failure to contribute to the realization of the vision just as much as is a failure to alter public structures.

This account is very formal and abstract. It would seem nearly irrelevant to the real historical situation if it were not for the effective existence of the feminist movement. In that movement, the unity of the personal and the political is being increasingly recognized in theory and realized in practice. This points to the meaningfulness and worthwhileness of proposing the ideal of spirit-centered wholeness.

A complete account of the ideal of spirit-centered wholeness would be impossible and even undesirable. But illustrations of how it is already being expressed will help to give some concreteness to the otherwise disembodied ideal. For some people of spirit, the all-determining cause is that of preventing massive starvation and providing food for the world hungry. The study of the causes and cures of the global food problem will lead to complex answers, but one among the causes will be the excessive consumption of meat, and especially beef, in affluent cultures. A natural response will be to reduce, if not eliminate, meat consumption. This response may be made by a spiritual person even at some risk to personal health.

If, however, the spiritual person orients life to a more inclusive vision, the personal embodiment of physical health will appear not only as a private *desideratum* that should be readily sacrificed to a larger cause but as a part of what is globally desirable. At the same time, it will not be assumed that there must be a trade-off between eating for one's personal health and eating in a way that is appropriate to the concern for world hunger. On the contrary, one will look for ways of eating that are appropriate to both at once. Once the question is posed in this way, it is not hard to find answers. Indeed, on the whole, the kind of eating that is inappropriate to a world of scarcity is also unhealthful for individuals, and the kind of eating that is good for individuals would be compatible with meeting the need for food of all people. The book *Diet for a Small Planet* expresses the unity of these concerns.

In other respects, such synergistic solutions are more difficult and complex. As long as we live in southern California, we find ourselves forced to choose between an immobility that would be personally and socially costly and involvement in a system of transportation that is outrageously expensive in terms of the resources of the world, appallingly destructive of our own environment, and alarmingly harmful to our health. We can buy smaller and more efficient cars and drive at more efficient speeds. But these are minor compromises rather than basic responses. Caught within the established system, no lifestyle is possible that is appropriate to the inclusive vision.

The alternative is first to conceive and then to create a different context for human living. This is not impossible. Paolo Soleri is far advanced in conceiving this different form of human habitat, and he is doing what he can to build an experimental model.

Soleri's city would simultaneously be far more frugal with respect to the earth's resources and far more humanizing in social relationships. It would restore the aesthetic dimension to our public lives and make our environment more healthful. If Soleri's cities were actually built, they could embody much of what we mean by spirit-centered wholeness. The general apathy toward his experiment is an indication of how little hold an inclusive vision has yet taken in our society.

The reference to this possibility provides an occasion for warning against a too optimistic view of the immediate relevance of the ideal of spirit-centered wholeness. Soleri is himself a fine embodiment of the spiritual ideal. His vision is extraordinarily comprehensive. It has led him to a relatively holistic style of personal life. Nevertheless, there remains a tension between the relative embodiment of the vision now and the price that must be paid if the vision is to be more fully realized. The quality of life that the city would make possible for those who lived in it cannot be enjoyed by those who are trying to build it. For them, sacrifice is necessary, including a sacrifice of wholeness.

Apart from these examples of how the comprehensive vision can express itself in ways that are beneficial simultaneously for the self and for the world, spiritual existence ordered to a holistic view is compatible with innumerable programs of self-improvement. Physical exercise, sensitivity training, consciousness-raising, various yogas, and many other disciplines are available and appropriate alongside traditional disciplines of study. Insofar as wholeness means the cultivation of all our potentialities, there is no limit to how far spirit-centered wholeness can go.

There is, however, a profound difference between spirit-centered wholeness and the wholeness described earlier. That wholeness involves a fullness of presence and spontaneity. If one practices some new discipline, it is not out of a need to be more inclusive but simply because at some point one finds this an attractive thing to do. Spirit-centered wholeness loses that spontaneity as it consciously orders and controls the personality. The wholeness it works to attain is not a given, embodied by those who refuse its disruption, but a conscious integration of many disciplined aspects of personal existence. Something precious has been lost.

The Possibility and Advantage of Spirit-Centered Wholeness

Given the negative character of this loss of spontaneity, it is not surprising that disciplines have developed for recovering it. The most serious and effective of these come from Zen. Zen can offer itself as an ideal lying beyond spirit-centered wholeness. The point here is that it is a different ideal and one that is realized through the overcoming of spirit. It is eminently appropriate for further investigation and evaluation, and, in my view, there are ways in which we may eventually move to some integration of the Buddhist realization of emptiness and spirit-centered wholeness. But that lies beyond this paper. Here we will consider the fulfillment of spirit-centered wholeness in Spirit-centered wholeness. This introduces the complex and controversial issue of the divine element in the world.

What makes spirit-centered wholeness unsatisfactory for many of us is its style of control. Because spirit-centered persons reflect about all aspects of their existence and how to order them, they are in position consciously to leave them undeveloped or to develop them in one direction or another. This can lead to a sort of self-manipulation or even self-construction that removes us a long way from the naturalness that is associated with real wholeness. It seems to turn the human being into an artificial product. It expresses the extreme extension of the mechanical world view, with the spirit placed in the position of the artificer. It is of a piece with human efforts to "master" all of nature and shape it to our will.

However, spirit-centered people have another option. Without abandoning their ability to think about this whole range of issues and to act according to their conclusions, they can turn from the stance of control to that of trusting service. This depends on acknowledging that there is something they do not control that is worthy of trust.

The two attitudes can be illustrated at many points. Some doctors think of the human body as a machine. When it malfunctions, they mend it. Other doctors see the human body as a mysterious and wonderful system that includes the power of self-healing and growth. When this power is blocked or inhibited, the doctor can intervene to remove obstacles to its working. But the doctor trusts and serves this healing power.

Similarly, some psychotherapists see themselves as the source of the cure they seek. By their skill and knowledge, they control the development of the patient. Other therapists believe that there is potentiality and power for health within the client or within the systems of relations between the client and others. The therapist's task is to act so that this healing power becomes more effective.

The same alternative exists in relation to what is going on within one's own body and psyche. One may perceive this activity as in itself neutral and directionless, so that the transcendent self decides for it and controls it. Alternately, one may see both body and psyche as embodying a tendency toward healthy growth. If one experiences life in this way, one may trust what is not within one's control and serve it.

The adoption of this latter attitude does not depend on the name given to that which one trusts and serves. One may call it Nature, or Life, or Creativity, or Eros, or Goddess. Here we will call it Spirit. What does matter is whether we believe that there is here a wisdom greater than our own that is worthy of our trust. If we do not, we will need to try to control events on the basis of our present understanding. If we do, we will be open to having our own understanding changed as we listen to the promptings of the Spirit.

If we do believe that there is trustworthy power and wisdom not in our control, the question of the right relation thereto becomes important. When this power is understood in certain ways, then passivity is encouraged. There is the idea, for example, that God is the potter and we are the clay. There is the notion of complete self-surrender. There is the slogan, "Let go and let God." But the Spirit is not a force outside other forces to which other forces including the human spirit should be subordinated. It is a power that operates only in and through other powers, to empower, to enliven, and to direct. Passivity is the refusal, not the acceptance, of its gift. But the image of co-working also fails. That too requires two separate powers acting together. What we need is an active acceptance of life or power, an active responsiveness to the directivity it contains. This entails rigorous thinking and vigorous acting in the public world. The attitude of trust does not reduce the energy with which we strive to realize our vision. But it does recognize the power that it trusts as at work everywhere even in those who oppose one's proposals, and it is open to the surprise that effective agents of the Spirit can be found in the most unlikely places.

Trusting the Spirit does not lead one to regard the "wisdom of the body" as infallible. But it does lead one to attend to the body and to take seriously what one hears when one does so. This may lead to the same regimen of diet, exercise, relaxation, and sleep that follows from the attitude of control. But it may not. One may learn of somewhat different needs if one listens to one's own very particular body. And in any case, the relation will be different. One will not be imposing on one's body what one has learned from other sources is good for the body. One will instead be guided by the body to give the body the chance to do what it wants and needs. Even when the requirement of the spirit necessitates the subordination of the body's claims, the denial of those claims will be with love and tenderness.

A similar change occurs at the level of spirit itself. The importance of the vision that orients all of life to purposes that are wider than oneself is not reduced. But it is now recognized that this vision itself is the gift of the Spirit. There is therefore a subtle but important shift in commitment. Instead of being committed finally to the vision and its implications for action, the commitment is directed toward the One who gave the vision.

This does not mean that one ceases to believe in the vision. One is no less sure that the people should be liberated or that the threat of war should be removed. But one does know that the vision is not absolute. The One who gave that vision can also enlarge and deepen it. In short, one is open to new insight and imagination. One will put oneself into those situations and those attitudes in which such new understanding is most likely to emerge. One will not suppose that apart from the gift of the Spirit one can produce them. One's own vision is not under one's control.

The attitude of trust in Spirit conduces to wholeness. It also makes the quest for wholeness less urgent. If one trusts the Spirit, one knows that one is all right as one is. One does not have to become whole in order to be all right. One is free to seek wholeness in service to the Spirit that makes for wholeness, because there is no need to become whole.

Trust in divine power is not a new idea in relation to the idea of spirit. Indeed, it is quickly suggested by the term, and most of the heroes of the spirit in the past have believed in God and trusted. The rise of spirit in history was closely related to belief in God; and in the writings of the apostle Paul, it is often difficult to distinguish spirit and Spirit. Unfortunately, for the most part, the way Spirit has been understood has not encouraged the quest for wholeness. It has more often encouraged the warfare of spirit with the flesh.

In spite of the differences between wholeness centered in Spirit and wholeness centered in spirit, the former remains a form of the latter. Wholeness centered in spirit is wholeness centered in the spirit that lives by trust in Spirit. Through that trust, Spirit itself becomes the center, but in doing so, it does not set spirit aside. It fulfills it.

Conclusions

Wholeness centered in spirit is not the only ideal appropriate to our time, but it is an important one. It cannot be attained by the expansion of a wholeness that lacks spirit. It can only be realized by a transformation and enrichment of the life of spirit. That requires that the vision out of which spirit orders human existence become inclusive and that we find ways to overcome the tensions between the fulfillment of the self and the needs of the whole. Finally, to overcome the centrality of control with its accompanying loss of spontaneity and presence, it is desirable that spirit identify Spirit and trust it.

10

The Identity of Christian Spirituality and Global Consciousness

Few Christians today defend either a personal piety that does not express itself in active concern for others or a social activism that is not nourished by a personal faith. "Evangelicals" call for social responsibility, and socially concerned liberals call for the renewal of spirituality. Yet there is danger that personal spirituality and public activity remain separate. They are often conceived as mutually supplementary, as if Christian life were a matter of putting together two aspects that inherently are unrelated. Spirituality is conceived as what is needed for us as individuals and in our relation to God, whereas social concerns are seen as the expression of this spirituality in relation to other persons, especially as these relations are mediated through institutions. The true wholeness of Christian existence is lost in this bifurcation, and it is not restored when the two sides are put together. The Bible knows no such separation of the inner and the outer, the vertical and the horizontal, the private and the public, the personal and the social. Christian spirituality is and can be nothing different from Christian faith, Christian life, or Christian existence. Christian life can be lived only in relations with other people, many

A public lecture presented on February 14, 1980, at the Ecumenical Institute for Theological Research at Tantur/Jerusalem, Israel, and published in the *Tantur Yearbook 1979-80*.

of which are mediated by institutions. The thesis of this paper is that Christian spirituality, and therefore Christian faith, life, or existence, today lead to and become global consciousness, and that to live an act in terms of global consciousness is to live and act as a Christian.

I will develop this thesis as follows. Section I discusses Christian spirituality as sensitivity and responsiveness to the divine Spirit that is God. Section II shows how this responsiveness leads to the strengthening of the human spirit. Section III argues that the self-transcendence that is involved in spirit produces global consciousness.

I

Christian spirituality is the formation of life in response to the divine Spirit as that is known in Jesus Christ. The divine Spirit is God. Hence, what we believe about God determines our spirituality.

In the popular spirituality of the English-speaking Protestant world, the predominant imagery of God has been influenced by Calvinism. God has been understood chiefly as transcendent personal will, and, accordingly, Christian spirituality has been the proper alignment of the human will to God's.

In one strand of this spirituality, the controlling belief is that the transcendent Creator and Ruler of all things has revealed his will only in his Word, which is fully and accurately recorded in the Bible. Christian spirituality is then primarily a matter of searching the scriptures to discover what God would have believers do and then conforming life and action to what is found. Prayer is chiefly a means of preparing oneself to find and obey the divine commands as they are revealed once and for all in the Bible.

In another strand of this spirituality, the emphasis shifts to conscience. God is understood to have created us with a free will and a mind capable of discerning right and wrong. Our task is to think clearly and to subordinate our private preferences to what we see to be right. In this view, the Bible provides useful illustrations as a way of broadening our understanding so that our judgment of right and wrong can be sharpened. Prayer is appropriate as a means of subordinating our selfish impulses to the divine purpose as that is grasped in the rational conscience.

When the accent falls on the omnipotence of God, the influence on spirituality is somewhat different. If God is omnipotent in the strictest sense—and many Christians, especially in the Calvinist tradition, have taught this—then whatever happens must be entirely in accord with God's will. This means that war and pestilence, suffering, and untimely death are willed by God as well as joy, peace, and love. The task of Christian spirituality is to enable us to see God's will in all things and to accept the most terrible events. In this view, the Christian is to be resigned to whatever happens. Prayer then helps us to overcome our rebelliousness against what happens and to acknowledge our infinite inferiority before the all-powerful one.

In another strand of popular spirituality, which shows more continuity with one branch of the radical Reformation, the Spirit is experienced as a kind of invasive force that displaces and replaces normal means of rational reflection and control. The current charismatic movement involves elements of this sort. For example, in the phenomenon of ecstatic speaking the normal, rational, and voluntary control of the vocal cords is replaced by a new control that is understood to be the divine activity in and through oneself. In general, self-determination is replaced by living in terms of the new directives that are received from the Spirit. In this view, prayer is primarily an emptying of self so as to become a channel through which the Spirit can move unimpeded.

Although the primary Christian imagery about God has stressed transcendence, there has also been a tradition of divine immanence. This tradition has been strengthened by the increasing influence of the great Asian religious ways. Here the divine is not viewed as so remote that it is known only through special acts of revelation in creation or historical self-disclosure. Instead, it is experienced as wholly immediate, present in the depths or heights of our own being, even identical with our true selves. Spirituality is then not so much crossing a chasm or becoming obedient but realizing what is always and everywhere already true and real, the universal presence of the divine. Usually, this is understood as an undifferentiated ground or depth of being, and true spirituality is an identification of ourselves with that ground or depth. The tendency is to direct attention away from concrete particulars to the supremely real. In this tradition, meditation is more fundamental than prayer. It includes techniques for disciplining the mind and freeing it from immersion in the finite.

The tendency of much Christian thinking about God to polarize around transcendent and immanent images has been partly checked by the Christian teaching of incarnation. The most distinctively and properly Christian form of spirituality is oriented to God as incarnate. The idea of incarnation implies that what is immanent is also transcendent and that what is transcendent is also immanent. The God who is fully and wholly present in the world is also the God who is always and everywhere transcendent of the world. That means that the God who is transcendent must be known in and through all things. It also means that what is known in the depths and heights of experience is not those depths and heights themselves but the transcendent God who is present there and everywhere.

If God is truly incarnate in the world, then our access to God is not limited to a book in which God has been revealed in the past or to a faculty given us in creation. God can be known in the here and now. But in identifying God in the here-and-now reality of our present lives, we must be guided by what has been learned in the past. As Christians we discern the incarnation of God normatively and decisively in Jesus of Nazareth. Because of him, we have learned to call the incarnate God Christ. To discern Christ in our world is to view the world through eyes that owe their vision to Jesus and to the response of the community of believers to his life, death, and resurrection. God is visible today only to the eyes of faith, but what is seen through the eyes of faith is not something esoteric, obscure, or remote, but the most basic reality of our lives and our world.

There are many ways in which the New Testament and the subsequent Christian community identify the presence and work in the world of the transcendent God. I will consider only one: life. Life, which is viewed apart from faith as simply a fact or an entity or a process, is experienced by Christians as grace, as gift, and finally as Christ's gift of Christ's self to us. All life is Christ's, but we recognize Christ most dearly in the enhancement, intensification, and fulfillment of life. Life is not something received at conception and then possessed by us. It comes as lure and threat, offering new possibilities, but demanding the surrender of established security. It is not transmitted out of the past but renewed as a gift. We do not exist apart from that gift but only within it, rejoicing in it or resisting it; for there is no such thing as life in general: There is only the particular livingness of each occurrence of life with its particular task and unique opportunity.

If we think of Christ as both the giver of life and the life that is, what form of spirituality is appropriate to this incarnational vision? It will be a spirituality that seeks to be sensitive to the concrete and particular character of the gift in each moment with its special tasks and opportunities. We will not orient ourselves to invasive forces but to the claim and possibility of life itself. In the discernment of the call forward that is the new offer of abundant life in each moment, we will be guided by our historical knowledge of God's past work in our tradition and elsewhere as well as by a rational grasp of general ethical principles, but in the end our need is for discernment in the sheer immediacy of each situation. Because of the endless possibilities of confusion and distortion, we need one another both for support and for criticism. The Quakers listen together and the Jesuits have means of testing the spirits. We have much to learn from both. The final test will be whether the results enhance life for others as well as ourselves.

II

Christian spirituality is the formation of life in response to the divine Spirit as that is known in Jesus Christ. This entails the enhancement, the intensification, or the fulfillment of life in ourselves and in others. The highest expression of life is experienced by Christians as the human spirit. Hence, the fullest response to the divine Spirit involves the fullest realization of the human spirit. Accordingly, forms of Christian spirituality vary not only with the understanding of God but also with the understanding of spirit.

One common understanding of the human spirit is as the vertical or depth dimension of human existence. It is associated with the mysterious, even the supernatural. It is sometimes associated with special states of consciousness to be cultivated by mystical disciplines. Although the exploration of such special states of consciousness is a promising frontier that we are invited to explore, spirituality in this sense is not essential to Christian life.

Sometimes the spirit is juxtaposed to matter as the most ethereal principle. Spirit is then seen as that aspect of human existence that is least dependent on its physical base. If the spirit in this sense is cultivated, ascetic practices may be used, or at any rate an attitude of contempt toward the body and the physical world is expressed. The Christian understanding of the physical body as created by God warns us against glorifying spirit in this sense.

The world of spirit also can be contrasted with the present world as the world that is to come. As believers, we are understood already to belong to that world in such a way that the conditions of this world do not bind us. Our home is there and we are merely sojourners here. The effect is usually again an ascetic spirituality, although it can also be license. Neither asceticism nor license reflects the Christian understanding of God's incarnation.

In the popular rediscovery of the importance of the emotional life in recent decades, spirit was sometimes paired with emotions and set against the reason and will that had repressed the human capacity to feel deeply and spontaneously. The resultant spirituality was one in which immediacy, emotional intimacy, and spontaneity of expression were successfully activated. At the opposite pole, reason and will are sometimes identified as the essential elements in spirit. In this case, the strengthening of spirit involves the control of spontaneous feelings and the direction of energies according to what are felt to be higher purposes. But the identification of spirit with either emotion or rational will leads to distortion.

Reinhold Niebuhr has taught us to think of the human spirit in a quite different way, one that is more illuminating of our tradition and our experience. Spirit is that aspect of our existence by virtue of which we transcend ourselves and take responsibility for ourselves. Spirit is mysterious in that we cannot pin it down or view it as simply one given part of the psychic life. However, the fact that people do transcend themselves in the way Niebuhr describes, and that Christian faith has encouraged this kind of transcendence, cannot be denied. Hence, though mysterious, the reality of the human spirit is evident.

It is spirit in this sense that is the highest expression of life in human beings. Life is itself always a process of going beyond given conditions. What merely repeats itself is inanimate, and where there is no life, inertia and entropy reign undisturbed. Life requires growth that in all its forms involves some element of novelty and transcendence. The more fully the human self transcends itself, the more fully it is alive. If the self identifies itself with established aspects of the psychic life, such as its desires or emotions, the full movement of life is blocked.

Consider a woman who identifies herself with her strong desire to have a proper family and home and in other ways to meet social expectations. Everything else is valued in terms of its contribution to meeting these goals. The goals themselves cannot be evaluated as long as she identifies herself with them. Only by disidentifying herself from these desires can she become free in relation to them, and therefore also free to respond to the new possibilities of life. In her freedom, she may choose to continue to pursue the same goals, but even then she would not be identical with them. She would be the self who chose them, a self capable of changing her goals.

Disidentification of the self from every fixed aspect of the psychic life is the negative way to attain and strengthen spirit. There are more positive ways. For example, one aspect of spirit is aspiration. Aspiration is the aim to become what one is not. This is quite different from desire, which is the aim to obtain what one wants. It is far more in accord with the movement of life that is continually going beyond what-is toward what-is-not-yet.

The self-transcending self can understand ideas with which it does not agree, and it can empathize with feelings that do not thereby become its own. It can have disinterested concern for others that is warm and personal without being governed by the attractiveness of the other or by expectations of return. Spirit can give freedom to emotions to express themselves without suppressing reason or will or permitting destructive action.

Spirit as self-transcending self also can liberate reason from what David Hume called its slavery to the passions. Hume thought that it is simply the nature of reason that it should be directed by human desires and used to support them and attain their ends. There is vast evidence that Hume was a shrewd observer of the human scene; for even the finest education and the greatest dialectical skill are no assurance that reason will not continue to serve the passions. Human desires for self-esteem or reputation can employ the most highly cultivated reason as well as the least developed. However, if the self identifies itself not with its passions, but with its transcendence of both passions and reason, then it can check the subordination of reason to passion and free reason to its proper end of conformation of thought to evidence.

III

I have criticized the idea of spirituality as the attainment of special states of consciousness such as mystical ecstasy. Christians need not seek altered states of consciousness, although we are free to do so if we wish. But spirituality as the cultivation of self-transcending does make us aware of ourselves and our world in new ways. It heightens or raises consciousness, and in this way it does produce new forms or shapes of consciousness.

When we are spiritually undeveloped or immature, we view reality unself-consciously and innocently from the perspective of the given self. Things are interpreted and appraised according to their effect upon oneself. One is, quite unqualifiedly, the center of one's world. That world may be highly inclusive—one may be conscious of what transpires in the farthest corners of the globe. But these events are viewed as they actually or potentially affect oneself.

Where self-transcending occurs, this simple egocentricity is broken, although, of course, it does not disappear. The person of spirit does not escape finitude or the distortions finitude introduces. But to whatever extent one views oneself from a perspective beyond oneself, one sees the disproportion between one's egocentricity and the actual situation as more objectively perceived. One sees that one is after all only one of many who all have their own perspectives, their equal claims and rights, as well as their own distorted perceptions.

The scope of the perspective in terms of which one relativizes one's own is appropriately correlated to the sphere within which one's actions have significant results. If what I am doing affects only my family, the perspective in which I act should be that of the family. I will need a family consciousness. If my actions have an effect on an institution or on a larger community, I will need to view them in this larger context.

The familial, institutional, or communal consciousness that self-transcending selfhood introduces in these cases is very different from tribal existence. In such existence, the individual exists only as a participant in the group. One derives one's being and meaning from the group so that one's interests are identical with the group interest. But in self-transcending selfhood, there is heightened capacity for independence from the group. The group-consciousness that is involved is a free adoption of a perspective that relativizes one's own, whether or not it is shared by anyone else. It is not immersion in the shared experience of the group.

Christian spirituality now requires of us a global consciousness. The globe has, in fact, been an interconnected system for a long time. But even as late as the nineteenth century, what mattered most to people was concentrated in relatively isolated sections of the globe. Only in the twentieth century have human affairs achieved a level of global integration that requires the consciousness of a unified history. Only in recent years has the interconnection with that history of events in the environment become sufficiently pressing to make urgent a consciousness that expands beyond the human. Today, we have no responsible choice but to develop a global consciousness that sees the web of life on the entire planet as affected by our actions.

Less evident than the spatial inclusiveness of the consciousness now required of Christians is the temporal scale. In what time frame should we interpret events? At one extreme is the dominant culture tendency to think in terms of a fiscal or academic year or a five-year plan, or, at most, a lifetime. At the other extreme is the possibility of placing events in the context of billions of years. The first tendency prevents us from dealing intelligently with current issues by blocking appropriate consideration of the effects of our actions on the foreseeable future. The second trivializes the importance of what occurs. I suggest that an appropriate global consciousness will concern itself with the history of life on this planet and see the present crisis in that overarching light. I suggest that it will be guided in its appraisals by the sense of the peculiar importance of the much briefer human drama in this total history. It will thus stretch our imagination to the limits but in such a way as not to belittle the importance of the issues we now confront.

Self-transcending selfhood opens us to new forms of consciousness in a second way. It enables us to see aspects of ourselves we had not noticed and to freely adopt a new attitude toward them. Education is partly an expansion of our information and an absorption of the values of our community, but it is also a way in which what is regarded as self-evident is rendered problematic and thus lifted into clear consciousness. Consciousness-raising points to this form of education, which is necessarily correlative with the strengthening of spirit.

Black consciousness came into being by lifting into clear consciousness the actual structure of relations between whites and blacks. Attention to these relations displayed them as based on assumptions about values, too often accepted also by blacks, which withered under examination. Instead of viewing blacks as persons who were to be evaluated according to their often unsuccessful efforts to embody the values affirmed by whites, their own values could be affirmed on an equal basis. The self-understanding of blacks was provided with a radically new possibility, and whites were introduced to a pluralistic consciousness. Other ethnic groups could follow the blacks into ways of viewing themselves in relation to the total society that refused to accept the standards and attitudes that had belittled their distinctive character.

Women have now performed a similar service. They have lifted to clear consciousness the actual structure of relations between men and women. They have thereby rendered problematic what had been simply taken for granted. Our inherited language and modes of interacting, our expectations of one another, and the social patterns that have expressed these are all now objectified aspects of ourselves and our communities. This means that we transcend aspects of ourselves that formerly, unconsciously, and apart from our choice governed us. This is further movement of life and spirit.

Perhaps the richest clarification of this type of consciousness-changing has been by Paulo Freire. He developed a pedagogy for the oppressed through which Brazilian peasants were enabled to name the oppressive elements of their world and thus to be in a position to challenge and change them. This conscientization is a process of moving into self-transcending selfhood.

If "global consciousness" were understood to mean only the spatial and temporal scope of the perspective in terms of which we view our actions and should not include also the deepening of this perspective through sociological criticism and self-reflection, then it would be profoundly inadequate. A true global consciousness is a way of viewing ourselves in global perspective that is progressively deepened and enriched by the heightening of awareness about features of the global situation of which we had previously not been aware. This is the consciousness toward which self-transcending selfhood moves. Any other form of "global" consciousness can only be one form of consciousness competing with others for Christian loyalty with no superior claim upon it. But an inclusive global consciousness is that at which Christian spirituality aims in our time, and global consciousness in this sense is Christian spirituality.

Christian spirituality as global consciousness must be distinguished from two other ways in which the global horizons of our existence are recognized. A military planner may think globally, but he does so in terms of the power and interests of his own country. He does not relativize the interests of his nation from a global perspective. Hence, he does not participate in global consciousness.

Global consciousness also differs from an ethics of global responsibility. Ethics appeal to our sense of obligation. As Christians, we all know that we ought to act for the good of all others as far as it lies in us. An ethics of global responsibility clarifies the possible and appropriate actions for us to take and emphasizes our obligation to take them. This is valuable and even necessary, but it does not involve a conversion of our basic perceptions or a reorientation of our basic attitudes. In short, it is not a new consciousness but only an extension of an old one. It is in danger of adding to our guilt more than it elicits right action. In contrast, global consciousness is a transformation of the way we see and understand our world, thereby altering our goals and purposes.

There can be no global consciousness without information. The information will be both about the needs of life throughout the globe and about the modes in which we are all interconnected. We will not advance to global consciousness, even should not, until we see that what occurs in the various parts of the globe is essentially bound together. Today, the information about our human interconnectedness, about the needs of our fellow human beings, and about the interrelationship between our species and others is readily available. But merely to have this information is not to enter global consciousness. Normally, the information is compartmentalized and brought to bear only on selected topics, or else "global problems" are added to a long list of concerns that the socially conscious person works on as time allows.

The test of whether global consciousness is becoming real is the extent to which patterns of interpreting events that are not obviously global are altered. For example, in what horizon of meaning does one view the threat of depression in the industrialized world? Normally, enlightened people have viewed the prospects of such a depression in terms of what depression will do to the lives of people in developed countries. Those who are particularly sensitive recognize that depression strikes hardest at the poorest and most powerless segments of society, and they dread it especially because of this. Viewed in this horizon, avoidance of a depression is of critical importance. The question is only how to avoid it, and how much sacrifice of other desirable goals (such as environmental protection, or preserving resources for posterity, or maintaining civil liberties) must be accepted in order to prevent the suffering of the poor. But if one views the situation with global consciousness, it is far more complex. Much of the global suffering and much of the threat to future generations stems from features of the First World economy. As long as that economy is strong, one may judge, those features will change but little. Perhaps Third World nations will have a chance to develop and gain true liberation only if the economy of the industrialized nations is seriously disrupted. Furthermore, one may see that the intolerable level of consumption of the world's nonrenewable resources and destruction of the planetary environment is due more to First World affluence than to any other one cause. Voluntary curtailment of consumption to the needed degree will not occur. Hence, a collapse of the present global economy may be the hope of the world.

I do not know enough to state that, in fact, a depression is desirable in global perspective. It may be that such a depression would lead to a war that would destroy the biosphere and with it human life, or, more moderately, that it would so upset international patterns of trade as to deny to the poorest nations the possibility of any development at all. The point is to illustrate the difference in ways of considering such questions that are introduced by a change of consciousness. When economic affairs are no longer viewed chiefly in terms of their consequences for the people of a few nations, but in terms of their effects on the whole planet, global consciousness has begun to take hold.

For many of us, it is even more difficult to enter into a changed consciousness with respect to personal matters than with respect to public events. For example, most of us men will quickly agree that women should have equal access to education and jobs and equal pay for equal work. It is another matter to deal with our own feelings of masculinity as these are bound up with cherished stereotypes of femininity.

Global consciousness operates in a similar way. At first blush, it seems less personally threatening than women's liberation. It seems that issues so vast are to be approached through international programs and national legislation. However, when we think more deeply, we discover that levels of consumption we consider moderate, even frugal, are utterly disproportionate to what is available to most of the world's population and that there is no possibility of rectifying this situation by raising others to our level of affluence. Viewing ourselves in global perspective, we discover that we are personally, as well as corporately, a part of the cancer that is destroying the planet. The changes that would be required if we were to cease to be a part of the problem are more radical than those required by a deep recognition of racism or sexism.

The real test of whether blacks or women have succeeded in raising our white male consciousness is at highly personal levels. To what are we committed? How centrally do the needs of the global poor, minority groups, or women operate among the purposes by which our lives are ordered? One of the problems we have felt in these areas is that the multiplicity of the demands laid upon us—rightfully and reasonably in each case—makes us distraught and ineffective.

The final test of our growth in Christian spirituality as global consciousness is how we view our own lives in their daily round. What commitments actually determine what we choose to do? Global consciousness has an advantage over the other forms to which self-transcending leads. It can function as a way to coordinate the implications of all the others. We cannot escape its demands by viewing it as one more cause alongside others and competing with them.

IV

The general argument of this paper is that truly Christian prayer alters the form or shape of the consciousness in terms of which we think and live, and that the direction of this change today is global consciousness. Prayer does this when it is in Jesus' name, that is, when it is not simply the verbalization of what we happen to desire but embodies the transcending and transformation of desire in the light of Christ. Prayer understood in this sense cannot be polarized in relation to social action, since its essential character is to reshape the perspective of all thought and action.

Similarly, the paper argues that truly Christian social action is the expression in action of the appropriate consciousness. It is not a matter of forcing oneself to conform to demanding moral principles. Such conformation is law. It is a matter of shaping goals of a Christianized and thereby globalized consciousness and acting so as to attain these goals. This is Christian freedom. It is not easy, or merely spontaneous, since the transcending of ecocentricity does not destroy that egocentricity. But as Christians, we identify ourselves and our purposes with the new creation of God that is our spiritual being rather than with the continuing desires of the flesh. To live from global consciousness is to express our true selves, not to subordinate ourselves to moral law.

But if all this is true, then we must confess that we are indeed babes in Christian spirituality. Honest self-examination must lead us to the conclusion that despite our traditional liturgies and our private prayers, our self-transcending has not led us very far. We continue to perceive our world and appraise events from the perspectives of particular groups and movements, usually those that provide us our personal identity. Verbally, we bring these, too, before God, and thus relativize them. But actually, our consciousness seems but little transformed by this act. Our conversion to Christ is partial and fragmentary.

There are many reasons for this, some of which can be classified under the old rubrics of original sin and natural depravity. But others point to particular weaknesses in the contemporary church and especially its failure to guide our spiritual formation in intentional and convincing ways. It may be that when we identify Christian maturity as global consciousness, we can more clearly order the disciplines of Christian life to that end.

11

Death and Dying: Individual and Planetary

Death has been a central topic for Christians from the beginning. In the first instance, this has been Jesus' death, but that death and the following resurrection have been understood in relation to human mortality generally. Death was seen by Paul as the final enemy.

Of course, the death of individual believers did not preoccupy the early church. It lived in anticipation of the imminent coming of the reign of God. Paul assured the faithful that those who died before the end would be resurrected to take part in that glorious day.

But as the expectation of a radical transformation of life on the earth faded, personal life beyond the grave assumed increasing importance. The dying and death that is the lot of all people was responded to by interpreting the sacraments as the medicine of immortality and viewing the Christian life as one of the deification, which meant, primarily, immortalization.

The contrast between the pleasures of this world that fade away and the everlasting joys of Christian salvation led to ascetic rejection of the world on the part of many. To encourage such rejection, death was emphasized. In view of the powerful attraction of this worldly enjoyment, only the deepest realization of its transitory character

---

An address given at the third International Conference on Buddhist-Christian Dialogue, Berkeley, California, August 1987.

165

could break attachment to it. This was often attained by concentrating attention upon dying and death.

In recent times, meditation on death has been recommended by Martin Heidegger in order to break concern for what others think. To realize deeply that we face death alone enables us to make our own decisions out of our own convictions and projects rather than to try to please others and win their approval.

Some Christian theologians have emphasized the ugliness and evil of death in order to magnify the greatness of the promise of eternal life. Others call us to face the fact of death realistically out of concern that its relative hiddenness in our time leads to a denial that ill prepares us for the reality.

Not all Christians have accepted the view that death is evil. For some, the assurance of a more blessed life beyond death has led to picturing death as a transition, one that is to be welcomed rather than feared. Especially those who have lived a full life and have lapsed into weakness and pain rejoice that death is at hand. They, too, find clear support in the New Testament.

The welcoming of death as a friend is not limited to those who are confident of blessedness hereafter. There are others who feel that death is as natural as life. Untimely death is evil, but death at the end of a good life is part of the good life, not something to be feared.

This sense of the goodness of death arises for many people when they are confronted with the possibility that medicine may some day put an end to the aging process. In principle, science may overcome physical mortality! Instead of rejoicing, many of us are appalled. What a horrible world we will have when we who are old no longer move on to make room for the young! Simone de Beauvoir depicted the horror of earthly immortality in her powerful novel *The Immortals*.

There is some biblical support for this view of death as friend. At least in the Jewish scriptures, the picture of the good life is one in which one dies after a long life productive of many descendants. There is usually no sense of evil associated with such death.

Despite this diversity of attitudes toward death among Christians, there is near consensus that the end of personal life on earth is a radically unique event. It is not simply an instance of some more general evil. It is not just one among the transitions and losses that constitute much of human life. Instead, it is incommensurable with all other events. The accent is on its stark finality.

This sense of the radical uniqueness of death arises from the assumption that personal identity from birth to death is a given. Death is the end of that personal career, at least on earth. There may be many losses and much suffering during the course of life, but they happen to a person who continues to exist and have new experiences. Death is the end of that road. The doctrine of the resurrection of the dead is affirmed against the immortality of the soul to emphasize the finality and evil of death despite confidence in life beyond death.

This strong conviction of a definite personal existence does not always fit well with the facts. There is endless debate as to when personal existence begins and ends. Does it begin with conception, with the first signs of fetal life, with a certain stage of the formation of the brain, with birth, with the beginning of language? All these answers are possible, and none are satisfactory. Similarly with death, it is not always easy to decide when personal existence has ended. Sometimes there is loss of memory, of recognition of others, and radical change of personality long before bodily death. Do we still take the death of the body as the radically decisive end? Surely, in fact, we will often have grieved over the loss of the person long before the heart stops beating. Nevertheless, these difficulties are felt as qualifications of the basic idea, not as indications that it has been wrongly conceived.

Buddhism offers a powerful alternative vision. For it, there is no given personal self that comes into being at some point and ends at another. Belief in such an underlying, substantial reality is an illusion that leads to suffering. The true self comes into being only as one becomes free of that illusion. It is the complete openness in each moment to all that is, an openness that is attained as one gives up clinging to the supposed reality of things as structured by our concepts and emotions. The true self is, hence, new and complete in every moment.

Of course, Buddhists know that there are continuities within the flow of experience. The doctrine of karma points out how what happens now is the result of what has happened in the past. But karma, even good karma, is to be overcome. This continuity that binds the present to the past is itself a consequence of the way we falsely construct our worlds.

Furthermore, at least for Buddhists in the Theravada tradition, the continuity among events in the life of a person here and now is not fundamentally different from the continuity between those events and future lives. As long as one is not free from illusion, the personal continuity endures. Death is not a major disruption. Certainly, it is not an ultimate evil. The evil is suffering, and the end of suffering is the end of personal existence. The true self is born when the illusory, personal existence ends. Thus, death as the end of personal existence is the birth of the true self. It is this death that is truly important and not the death that is the mere cessation of biological life.

As a Christian, I find that I have much to learn from Buddhism on this point. There is no substantial person underlying the flow of experience. Personal existence is not all or none but rather more or less. The memories and continuities of personality that constitute personal identity are continuously coming into being and passing away. My personal being begins to die as soon as it begins to live. By freeing myself from a false hypostasization of myself, I can indeed attain greater freedom and openness, fuller relatedness to others. I also can see the death that comes with the last breath and the cessation of the beating of the heart as less drastically different from the dying that is part of all living. It, too, I can let occur in its due season.

Yet, I am not attracted to all features of Buddhist thought on dying. One reason death has loomed so large in Christian thought has been the conviction of the goodness of the created order. Life, even very ordinary life, is a great good. We know that it is corrupted and filled with suffering, but we affirm it, even in its corrupted form, as worth enjoying.

Also, we see in the continuities that pervade the flow of personal experience something positive. Experience can become richer because of the accumulation of experience. Understanding and wisdom can grow. Memories can bring to the present balance and contrast that enhance experience.

This is not to deny that personal existence is replete with sorrow and suffering. But the fundamental Christian judgment is that it is nevertheless good as the created order in general is good. To understand that personal existence is a construct rather than an ontological given can enable it to be better. It need not bring it to an end.

In short, I want, as a Christian, to celebrate the ambiguous values of the ordinary with all their mixtures of joy and suffering. I want to orient my life and activities to the increase of joy and the decrease of suffering, but I see this as always a matter of relative gains and losses, never as the eradication of suffering. Further, I cannot see that the kind of continuity among events in personal existence in this life could characterize their relation to events in a future life on earth or on some other planet. Biological death seems more determinative, more final, than the Buddhist vision suggests. And untimely death is a tragic evil.

The Buddhist analysis rightly relativizes biological death so that it cannot be the final enemy. But a Christian thought experiment can also relativize suffering. Consider a world devoid of life. In such a world there would be no suffering, and in one sense there would be no evil. Yet, if a world teeming with life were possible, then the occurrence of a dead one would seem to be a very great evil indeed.

To me, indeed, the dying and death of the planet is the true candidate in our time for the role of final enemy, or supreme evil. Such dying and death includes much suffering and many personal deaths, but it transcends these in its significance. It is not simply the addition of individual cases. It has a finality they lack.

That the planet would some day die has been known for a long time. But the information that some billions of years in the future the sun's energy would cease to suffice for life on the planet pointed to an event too remote to be of much concern. A few billion years is, from the perspective of human time, almost equivalent to forever.

The dropping of the atomic bomb on Hiroshima initiated a profound change. The collective consciousness gradually assimilated the realization that technology now existed that could destroy life on the planet. It became clear that this was no longer a matter of a remote and unimaginable future but of an imminent threat. We might ourselves be part of the dying of the planet. Even if it survived us, it could do so only under the threat of death. Beside this inclusive death, the deaths of individuals pale into relative insignificance.

This relativization of individual, personal death does not lead us to grieve less at the loss of a friend or sorrow less when potential leaders, who might have helped redirect us, are cut down at the height of their powers. Nor does it lead to lessened anxiety about personal mortality. But it adds a context in which the meaning of personal death, and of personal life as well, is changed.

Although the possibility of the death of the planet became evident with the advent of the nuclear age, and although this has provided a new context for the understanding of all suffering and death, it has been possible to hope that the utter devastation of a major nuclear war can be indefinitely postponed. Mad though we human beings are, it seems possible that the awareness of the ultimate horrors to be inflicted on all sides in such a war may continue to deter the use of these weapons. There is no ground for confidence, but there has been no need for hopelessness.

In my case, the deeper threat to hope has come from the awareness that even apart from such a war, human activity is destroying the planet. We are poisoning the air, the water, and the soil. Our heating of the atmosphere will cause the rise of ocean levels exacerbated by the melting of the solar icecaps, as well as catastrophic climatic changes. The ozone layer that has protected the biosphere from damaging rays of the sun is being reduced. Topsoil is pouring into the sea. Nuclear wastes are placing posterity in permanent danger. Species are disappearing at a rapid rate. On and on. The biosphere is already dying and its capacities for self-renewal are being pressed beyond their limits. Only drastic changes in human behavior would slow this process, and instead our self-propagation becomes still more rapid and our quest for greater consumption continues unabated. The awareness of a present and actual dying, already well advanced, affects me more deeply than the threat of a sudden death that *may* be indefinitely postponed.

It is, of course, an exaggeration to say that the dying and death of the biosphere is the *ultimate* evil. We can at least imagine something more evil. We can imagine that there are living planets elsewhere in the universe and that all of them are dying. That would be a more ultimate evil than the death of this one.

The meaningfulness of life here and now is far more deeply threatened for me by the awareness that the whole biosphere is dying than by the knowledge that I am personally dying. The latter leaves open the sense that I can contribute to others, that living things will continue to make their contribution to God, that God's purposes are yet working their way out in nature and history whether or not I can discern them clearly.

But if it is all dying, it is harder to see the point of living. There are no scenarios to be imagined in which my efforts could contribute to a better future. Meaning must be found either in the hope that the dying can be stayed or in the immediacy of enjoyment here and now—or in some combination of the two.

On a dying planet, it is hard to know how to speak, what to say, to the children who seem doomed to take part in that dying. They need hope, both for their own lives and for the context apart from which their lives lack significance. But it often seems their only choices are to ignore the truth and live blindly, or to face the truth and despair.

Neither Christianity nor Buddhism seems prepared to address this evil. Christians sometimes affirm that God will not let the global death occur. Before the dying process has gone all the way, there will be an intervention. Supernaturally, a new age will be brought into being discontinuous with this one.

This message may save those who believe it from despair, but only at the price of denying the seriousness of the real situation. Conclusions can be drawn from it that hasten the dying process. For if God will intervene before we must pay the price for our murderous acts, then proceeding with the killing will do us no harm; it may even hasten the intervention of God.

Alternately, Christians call for the full acceptance of human responsibility for the fate of the earth. We say that God has limited the exercise of divine power to make space for the exercise of human freedom and that all depends upon how we assume the responsibility thus placed upon us. This encourages a realistic assessment of the crises and commitment to take action to meet them.

But this call to action does little to mitigate the threat of despair. Measured by the dimension of the crises, the positive efforts in which we collectively are now engaged are small indeed and often at cross purposes. The principalities and powers that continue to kill are too entrenched to be much affected by heroic actions. While skirmishes are won here and there and the destructive forces are held at bay, elsewhere new patterns of murder become evident. Further, each finds within herself or himself how powerful are the habits by which we support the power of destruction even when we consciously commit ourselves to life.

The dominant Buddhist ethos seems no more helpful. Much Buddhist teaching has been developed for the purpose of disengaging human concern from mundane matters. One technique has been to emphasize how vast are the reaches of space and time, how trivial are the matters that loom so large for us. Even the destruction of this planet is made to appear a detail in the whole cosmic sweep of things. Also, the sense of beginnings and ends is replaced by a feeling of the endless ongoings of cosmic process. The end of one planet as a locus of life does not have, in this vision, a strong note of finality.

In this way, the Buddhist may be saved from both unrealistic expectations of divine intervention and a moral responsibility that leads to despair. But if one is freed from those dead ends by adopting a less-engaged relationship to the events of our time, they cannot be simply a gain. Change depends on rigorous analysis of the causes of the dying and examination of alternative scenarios of political action that might slow down or reverse it. The general Buddhist analysis of the causes of suffering helps but little. There is danger that what one will find in Buddhist practice is release from the torment of hope and hopelessness in an a-historical way of thinking, just when it is most urgent to focus attention on history.

Thus far, I have been questioning the ability of either Christianity or Buddhism to respond effectively to that dying and death that is most important for us to consider now. The current popularity of the topic of death and dying with its continued focus on the individual reflects the psychological need to focus attention on where our cultural resources have something to contribute rather than to turn to those more fundamental issues on which we have so little to say. Nevertheless, both Buddhists and Christians can contribute to the understanding and response to the dying and death of the planet as well.

Consider first the crucial contributions that Buddhism can make. Buddhist meditation can reduce the preoccupation with self that inhibits attention to the inclusive problem and distorts actions for good causes. It can also open us to the interconnectedness of all things and break us out of our age-long dualistic habits of thinking. It can reduce our attachment to possession and consumption and enable us more realistically to appraise the issues and the proposed solutions. Joanna Macey has demonstrated the fruitfulness of these Buddhist contributions in empowering concerned people to work more effectively for peace.

Even more impressive is the Sarvodaya movement in Sri Lanka under the leadership of A.T. Ariyaratne. Meditation here, as in Joanna Macey's case, is employed not as a step toward ultimate complete enlightenment as much as it is a means to enable believers to work effectively on the most pressing issues of our time. It has also been the Buddhist vision, strengthened in meditation, that has shaped the definition of the task, guided and motivated workers, and won the serious participation of hundreds of thousands of ordinary villagers.

To understand the significance of this Buddhist contribution to pushing back the death-dealing forces of the world, we need to consider briefly the situation in Sri Lanka. While most of the Third World joined the international economy in the years after World War II, hoping thereby to attain Western levels of affluence, Sri Lanka did not. It continued to export tea grown on colonial plantations, but instead of seeking to expand trade and to industrialize, it gave priority to providing its citizens with food, basic medical care, education, and cheap transportation. This expressed a mixture of values from Buddhism and Western humanist socialism.

The result was that judged by per capita gross national product, Sri Lanka fared very poorly, but judged by social welfare standards, such as the Physical Quality of Life Index, it did very well. This index measures literacy and life expectancy, and Sri Lanka attained standards in these areas much higher than Third World countries that concentrated on economic progress.

But this combination of Western socialism and Buddhism finally failed. The nation could not afford the welfare programs, especially because it had to import rice to feed its people. Two roads were open to it. There was a Buddhist proposal that saw the failure in terms of neglect of the village life that was the basis of Sri Lankan society and economy. Food had been provided to all by keeping the price low. That had discouraged peasants from growing rice. Also, centralized power led to dependency and the loss of community in the villages. The solution was to restore the villages to health. This meant empowering people to analyze their own situations and to develop local economies they could understand and control. These economies were to be close to the soil, concerned with the natural environment, and based on technologies the peasants understood. Specifically, it meant restoring the irrigation ponds, many of which had been destroyed by the British for the purpose of disrupting and disempowering the colonized people.

The other solution was for Sri Lanka to join the global economy. That meant exploiting its human resources of cheap labor and its natural resources of timber and water, attracting international capital, and industrializing. Specifically, it meant building a huge dam for electricity and massive irrigation. And it meant shifting to production for export at the price of an unsustainable agriculture.

I suppose it is not necessary to tell you which policy won. It was the latter, of course. The westernized Sri Lanka elite worked with international development leaders to plan the future for Sri Lanka. The dam has been built. The land is deforested. The soils are eroding. The problems of feeding the people of Sri Lanka in the future is exacerbated.

The Buddhists, however, rightly realizing that there was no long-term hope for Sri Lanka through westernization, continued, unaided, their program of village development. Thousands of villages have been helped to help themselves; so, in spite of government policies that work against it, a healthy rural life exists, one that may survive even the collapse of the multinational system of trade. Perhaps also it may save enough of the Sri Lankan ecology to stave off the threatening holocaust there too.

Christian faith also makes important contributions to an adequate response to the dying of the planet. Alongside the call to responsible action, which can so easily burden the Christians beyond endurance, there is the assurance of the grace both of empowerment and of forgiveness. Christians can experience God's help and guidance and know that, while their best efforts are still tainted by sin, their sin is forgiven and their efforts are affirmed by God. Even worldly failure is not finally failure if it is offered to God as our best.

Christians are encouraged by our faith to view the present situation in light of where it comes from and to what end it is headed. This supports a critical analysis of the social-historical-cultural-religious factors that are now operative along with sustained reflection upon them. It also encourages imaginative visions of possible futures worth working for. These futures may be quite different from anything that has ever occurred in the past.

I shall take Teilhard de Chardin as a representative Christian thinker. I select him for two reasons. One is that setting his vision over against that of the Buddhist Ariyaratne reveals its one-sidedness and failures, but also its vivid contemporary embodiment of the distinctive strengths of the Christian tradition. The second reason is that a disciple of Teilhard is making concrete proposals for responding to the dying of the planet that are radically different from those of Ariyaratne, but still, in my opinion, of profound positive significance. I refer to Paolo Soleri.

Whereas the Sarvodaya movement in Sri Lanka aims at the renewal of traditional village life, Paolo Soleri proposes an urban habitat for the future. Whereas the Buddhist vision of Ariyaratne emphasizes human community on a small scale and the intimate interdependence of humanity and nature, the Teilhardian vision of Paolo Soleri aims to take the next step in the evolutionary development of humanity.

Soleri sees that the way cities are now built generates problems that cannot be solved and can be alleviated only by heroic efforts. As cities spread out over larger and larger areas, much of the world's best farm land is paved over. In each generation, a larger population must be fed on a smaller agricultural base. Meanwhile, urban sprawl separates the various ethnic and economic segments of our society from one another, increases concern for private possession and consumption, and reduces willingness to support public facilities. The spirit of citizenship declines. Further, for an increasing number of urban dwellers, the countryside becomes remote, accessible only in major expeditions.

Cities of this sort are extremely consumptive of resources. First, they require complex transportation systems with major emphasis on the private automobile. The drain on nonrenewable energy sources is enormous. Secondly, the cost in natural resources of extending public utilities and services over these vast areas is huge. Those who do not own a car are limited in mobility, and those who cannot afford the rising costs of public transportation and utility bills are reduced to a level of isolation and misery rare in traditional societies. In most Third World countries, cities simply are unable to extend utilities to the inrushing populations of slum dwellers. Cities of this sort breed crime, disease, and drug addiction. The costs go on and on.

One response to the depressing future of the cities is that of the Sarvodaya movement of which I have spoken. By renewing healthy village life, the forced migration to huge urban centers would at least be slowed. There would be a better chance that services could be extended to newcomers and that utter squalor could be avoided.

But it may be that human imagination can envision a future that is not one of simply fending off decay. If so, new types of urban habitat must be conceived, and it is to this task that Soleri has devoted himself. What kind of urban habitat can renew prideful participation in city life, concern of the public, freedom from abject poverty, and a healthy relationship between city and countryside, the artificial and the natural?

Soleri's proposal is an architectural ecology or arcology. An arcology would be designed so as to take maximum benefit from the sun. Ideally, passive solar energy would supply all its needs! This would be achieved in part by a great reduction of those needs. For example, the huge quantity of energy used in contemporary cities for transportation would be cut to a small fraction. Within the arcology there would be no motor transportation. Also, the arcology would be designed so that waste heat from industry would supply the energy required for heating and cooling the remainder of the structure.

Both of these changes would be achieved by conceiving of the arcology in three-dimensional terms. This would make it possible to locate industry beneath the other segments of the city and easily capture its energy for other purposes without wasteful transmission systems. It also would greatly reduce distances between parts of the city. This compression of space would be greatly facilitated by the abolition of motor transportation, since more than half the surface in many parts of present cities is devoted to the car and bus. Given the much smaller distances to be traversed, elevators, escalators, and moving sidewalks would suffice alongside paths for bicycles and pedestrians and steps for walking. Rich and poor would have equal access to all parts of the city.

Most of the land now covered by cities would be returned to other uses, chiefly agricultural and recreational. The poor could share free access to this rural environment since it would be only a few minutes by foot from any part of the arcology. In Soleri's vision, a system of hothouses would both provide much of the food for the arcology and also help to capture the solar energy needed by the city.

My topic is death and dying and not scenarios for urban habitat; so I will refrain from further describing Soleri's vision. My justification for introducing it here, along with that of Ariyaratne, is that both point the way of life in a dying world. Whereas neither Buddhism nor Christianity in their major expressions is able to face the reality of this dying, and both still prefer to concentrate on the individual person's suffering and death, both also are able to provide impulses that are genuinely relevant, indeed far more hopeful than those coming from the general culture, or from the tradition of the Enlightenment nurtured in universities, think tanks, and national bureaucracies.

Honesty impels me to acknowledge that the symmetry I have tried to suggest is imperfect. Whereas Ariyaratne is fully explicit about his commitment to Buddhism and the Buddhist sources of his thought and work, Soleri denies that he is a Christian. Hence, I must say a word about my refusal to take that denial seriously. This man who denies that he is a Christian is also an avowed and committed disciple of Teilhard de Chardin. He is now building the Teilhard cloisters and hoping that he can find a monastic order to share his city with him. The Christianity he rejects is the Italian Catholicism of his childhood, which he experienced as repressive and moralistic. For him the "Christian" God is the author and defender of the origins and the one who opposes every expression of human venture and creative freedom. The God of the future is, in his imagination, something utterly different. Yet we all know how strong the eschatological and even apocalyptic note has been, and now is, in Christianity. Hence, having acknowledged the importance to Soleri of berating what he understands to be Christianity, I hope you will allow me to continue to affirm that his vision stems from resources within eschatological Christianity.

It is all too easy for those who see hope for the renewal of Third World rural villages to be unsympathetic to a vision of towering cities. It is equally easy for those who are focused on the novel solution to novel problems employing the latest technology to be contemptuous of the efforts to revitalize past forms of rural life. This is but a specific form of the difficulty of genuine mutual appreciation between Buddhists and Christians.

But the time for mutual rejection and claims of superiority is past. In a world in which almost all the dominant forces, including those dominant among Buddhists and Christians, are actively or passively participating in the killing of the planet, the time has come for enthusiastic mutual support among those few who are genuinely on the side of life. Buddhist eyes and Christian eyes have been conditioned to look in different directions to see what makes for life. But that does not mean that their conclusions and their proposals, however different, are contradictory. They are complementary. We need both. Rural and urban life are both important. Traditional societies and new urban habitats can both support life in a way that our dominant present society cannot.

In the midst of my critique of both Buddhism and Christianity for their general inability to shift their directions so as to be truly relevant to the most important dying and death of our time, I also have made bold positive claims for them. It is my considered judgment that they have inspired the most hopeful responses to the dying of our world, the most practical programs for the strengthening of life. Now I want to make a stronger claim. I believe that to whatever extent each is faithful to its deepest commitments and their meanings in our time, it will repent of its irrelevance and throw its energies into the struggle for life.

There are tremendous obstacles to this shift. Although both work for life, they are accustomed to doing so at levels that distract their energies from the larger task. The Buddhist concentration on the enlightenment of the individual and the Christian concentration on personal death and on social justice are both laudable in an unthreatened world. But commitment to these efforts as ends, rather than as means to a more urgent end, inhibits relevance to the fundamental task. On a sinking ship, neither psychotherapy nor the organization of underpaid stewards is the best way to expend one's energies—except as it is genuinely contributory to preventing the sinking.

I am convinced that enlightenment on the one side and faith in Christ on the other, when fully realized, entail commitment to life and to what must be done for the preservation and renewal of a living planet. They do so in quite different ways and continue to orient us to different aspects of the problem, to different elements of the solution. We need one another. Let us celebrate our differences. And if we must compete, let us compete in our gratitude to one another, our openness to transformation by one another, and our contributions to the revitalization of the planet.

12

In the Beginning God Created

When people consider the care of the earth, one good place to begin is at the beginning. Where did the earth come from? Why is it here? What is its nature and purpose? And when Christians consider the care of the earth, the best place to begin to answer these questions is the beginning of the Bible, the first chapter of Genesis.

The primary image of the first verse of the chapter is that of God creating the earth out of the void, the formless. This cannot mean that there first existed a formless matter apart from God's creative activity that then later was given form, for whatever exists must have some form, and that form is not possible apart from God. Nothing has ever existed apart from God's creative act.

The image communicated by the chapter as a whole goes further. God is pictured as bringing into being richer and richer forms, or formed things, culminating in human beings. God is, then, not simply the reason that there is something rather than nothing. God is also the reason that there is progressive ordering and enriching of the earth. And at the summit of God's creative work, at least on the planet Earth, stands humanity!

The importance of human beings to God is clearly and powerfully affirmed. For Christians, the care of the earth should be, above all, the care of human beings, and the attention of Christian thought and practice has rightly focused here throughout the centuries. Again and again, the Scriptures testify to God's concern for humanity and especially for the poor and powerless. They forbid us to lose sight of the question of justice even when human survival is at stake, whether it is threatened by nuclear war or by ecological holocaust. The survival worth seeking is survival with justice, and a profoundly unjust world is inherently unsustainable.

Nevertheless, as so often happens, an appropriate focus has become an exclusive concern. What is very important comes to be treated as alone important. The finite and creaturely human good is absolutized. The result is idolatry. We humans, and especially we Westerners, have made humanity an idol.

This violates our biblical faith in two ways. First, it arrogates to humanity what is true only of the Creator. Second, it leads us to neglect the rest of God's creation, especially the rest of the earth.

Too often, Christians have read the biblical creation story as if it told us that the earth existed only for human benefit, as if the remainder of the earth were of no value in itself or for God apart from us. But the text does not say that. Before and quite apart from the arrival of human beings, God rejoices in the creation. Again and again, God *sees* that it is good. That means that it is good in itself as God has created it and it is also good for God.

How carefully the story makes this point and then goes on to make another! Only after the creation of human beings does God see that the earth is *very* good. But note: God does not see that human beings by themselves in separation from all other things are "very good." Instead, it is the earth in its totality, replete with all sorts of living things, *including human beings*, that is very good.

What does this mean for the Christians' care for the earth? It means that our care should be for all the creatures God has made. In contemporary language, biodiversity is good, and it is our responsibility to avoid the wanton extinction of species. It means also that our care should be for ourselves in our interconnectedness and interdependence with all these creatures.

These conclusions seem to some in tension with the divine command to subdue the earth and have dominion over the other creatures. There is certainly tension between recognition of the intrinsic value of other creatures and of their diversity, on the one hand, and some of the interpretations of human dominion that have characterized Western thinking. But today, we are realizing that these interpretations expressed human arrogance more than biblical teaching. The Bible frees us to use the earth to meet our needs, especially for food, and God commands us to be fruitful and to multiply. However, this commandment to us supplements the same commandment to other living things; it does not authorize us to prevent them from fulfilling God's purpose! If any one species multiplies indefinitely at the expense of the others, God's intentions are thwarted. If we are to represent the divine dominion on earth, this does not entail displacement, exploitation, and destruction of our fellow creatures but rather responsible concern for the health and well-being of the whole biosphere or ecosystem, including humanity.

This sensitive balance of understanding can be highlighted by comparing it with other views of the earth operative in the contemporary world. Of these, the most widespread will employ the metaphor of the machine. Most scientific formulations still use mechanistic models even though these have broken down at crucial points.

The model of the earth as machine includes its intrinsic value. A machine is valuable to its user, but in itself, apart from any use by another, it is valueless. When the model is extended to include human beings with the cosmic machine, questions of value are either silenced or removed to another sphere of discourse.

On the other hand, when the machine metaphor is taken to describe only the nonhuman world, and human beings, or at least human minds, are located outside the machine, value can be attributed to them, and the earth can be viewed as valuable for humanity. The result comes close to the absolutization of humanity noted above as resulting from a misreading of Genesis. Indeed, the misreading of the Bible and the influence of modern scientism have often reinforced one another.

This tendency can be checked when the doctrine of creation is retained. Indeed, at its origin, the model of the machine was supported partly to accent the need for a Creator. Machines are themselves manufactured, and a cosmic machine was thought to require a cosmic maker. Here the Genesis pattern is maintained, except that the intrinsic goodness of the earth even apart from human use and enjoyment is omitted. Often, ruthless exploitation is encouraged.

Among those who have recognized that the world as a machine is a metaphor and not literal truth, some have gone on to argue that all the ways in which human beings envision the world express their conditioned perceptions and imagination rather than something objectively given. They have refocused attention from the objectively given world to human language and the way in which language constructs the human world. In its extreme form, this line of thought denies that here is an objective world at all. Instead, there are the world constituted by human language and imagination. In this view, whatever can properly be meant by "world" is finally a creation of the human spirit.

A large part of human thought today moves between two extreme views. For some, the world is objectively real, machine-like, and self-explanatory, requiring no reference to a Creator. For others, the world (or each of the many worlds) is constituted by human language and imagination. Here the world is created, but by the human spirit, not by God.

The biblical view stands in marked contrast to both. In philosophical language, it asserts that the world is contingently real. It exists in itself and for God apart from human interpretation and valuation. But it is not self-sufficient or self-explanatory. Its existence and its character cannot be understood apart from God's creative activity. That creative activity consists of calling into existence new forms of being that heighten the world's value. Human beings are among the contingently real entities who are called by God to achieve new values as well as to sustain old ones. How we respond to this call has become decisive for the fate of the whole earth.

This sense of the radical contingency of both the being and the destiny of the earth accentuates the concern for its care. We have learned how remarkable is the achievement of God on this planet. The earth could so easily not have been, or not have been able to generate life. Only a little difference in the universal patterns of order established in the big bang, and life would have been impossible. Also, in the course of its emergence and transformations, how easily matters could have gone awry! How beautiful, how wonderfully intricate, is the web of life fashioned over these billions of years! We, too, see it with fresh eyes and see that it is good. And when we view ourselves as a part of the web of life, we see that the whole is very good indeed.

We see also that it is very fragile. Its future is as contingent as its past. Now it depends not so much on physical, chemical, and biological conditions independent of human action but precisely on that action itself. Will people shift from exploitation of the earth for short-term profit to care for the earth for its future inhabitants and for God? Will national interest in political power be subordinated to the human interest in a rich and healthy biosphere? Can actions restrain themselves from the supreme madness of Mutually Assured Destruction?

In the language of the first chapter of Genesis, we human beings are created in the image of God. In the language of Paul, we are fellow workers with God. Perhaps being in the image of the creator means that we participate in the work of creating. Certainly, this seems to be the case. Because of the human use of tools, our role in shaping and reshaping the earth is massive. We have been right to emphasize our creative powers.

But in the Bible, whatever creative role is assigned us is always in the context of the primacy of God's creating. In modern times, human beings have forgotten this. We have tried to assume the primary role in creating, treating God's creation as mere resources for our re-creating.

Instead of working *with* God's present creative working, we ignore it. The result is that we replace the natural, living environment with an artificial and inanimate one. We try even to recreate ourselves rather than opening ourselves to God's creative working within us. The price we are paying for this self-idolatry is high. The proper care of the earth requires a basic shift from the stance of manipulation and control to one of working with the forces of life to enhance and liberate them. Today, it entails the lessening of human pressure in much of the planet.

Rightly understood, our participation in creative activity does not place us in competition with God. God does not create as one being alongside other beings. The image of a huge person outside the universe and creating it as a human being makes a toy simply cannot work. God is creatively present everywhere, acting in and through all things. Human freedom, human imagination, human creativity, are all aspects of God's creative working. God creates in and through all the other creatures of the earth as well.

Because God creates in and through creatures that are not mere automata, creatures that as real, contingent beings participate in determining what they become, the earth, for all its goodness, is imperfect. All creatures, and especially human creatures, have freedom to resist God's creative purposes and to redirect our contingent creative capacities to destruction. God calls us to that true freedom that is found in genuine openness, in full responsiveness, to one another, to all the creatures, and to God, but to some degree, always, we resist, and sometimes, spectacularly, we rebel.

If we cannot image God as a great and powerful being, external to the creation, manipulating it from without, what image can we use? Sally McFague has recently renewed the proposal (one that has long been important to Charles Hartshorne) that we think of the world as God's body. Like all metaphors, this one has its limits, as McFague well knows. But it has the virtue of highlighting the intimacy of the relation of God and the world. What we do to a manufactured object may or may not be particularly important to its maker. But what we do to a person's body, we do to that person. That can never be a matter of indifference. When we view the world as God's body, we cannot doubt that what we do to one of the least of the creatures, not to human creatures alone, we do to God.

The image of the world as God's body comes close to that of Mother Earth. That image has inspired in many peoples a reverence for the earth, a reluctance to injure or violate it. There can be little doubt that the biblical imagery of creation was developed in part to counter this divinization of the earth itself. The earth is not God, and human beings should not hesitate to reshape the earth as this helps to meet human needs. In caring for ourselves, we are caring for the earth even when that means digging minerals out of the ground. The Christian use of the metaphor of the world as God's body must maintain the possibility of differentiated evaluations that was opened up by the de-divinization of the earth.

The point is important because, in reaction to the idolatrous excesses of exploitation of nature and indifference to the well-being of other creatures, the re-divinization of the earth is gaining adherents. For some it seems the only way to ground the concern for the care of the earth, and for them it often means the rejection of gradations of value and discriminating evaluations. Some "deep ecologists" insist that any judgment that some creatures are of greater worth than others can only be a continuation of the disastrous anthropocentrism of our recent past. In their view, human beings may especially look out for their own species, because that is what is natural for members of any species to do, but this natural behavior can never be justified on the grounds of superior human importance or value. Objectively, everything that is has the right to be, no one thing more than another. Even the notion of human responsibility of the care of the earth is set aside as an expression of human arrogance.

The biblical vision is quite different. All creation is good in itself and for God. The image of the world as God's body vivifies the immediacy of the contribution each creature makes to God as well as suggesting how intimately all are bound up with one another. Still, God's body is not, as such, God. God is Spirit. And although all parts of God's body are good, they do not all contribute in equal measure to God. There *are* gradations of value. Every sparrow has value in itself and for God, but a human child is worth many sparrows. And it is not mere anthropocentrism to believe that a porpoise is worth many tuna, or a whale, many squid.

Albert Schweitzer agreed with the deep ecologists in an important respect. His reverence for life did not allow in principle for judgments that some living things are of greater worth or importance that others. Yet, in practice he continually made judgments of this sort, feeding fish to birds and killing bacteria for the sake of human health. Since practical judgments are inescapable, is it not better to reflect on the grounds on which they can be made?

To see the earth as creation, existing contingently, dependent on God as well as being intimately related to God, frees us to think critically about activities that inevitably destroy as well as support life. In Whitehead's language in *Process and Reality* (p. 105), all "life is robbery" and "the robber requires justification." *What* may we kill *when* in order to satisfy our wants? When does our killing transgress all justifiable bounds? Those who believe the whole earth is God's creation cannot escape these questions. They are not always easy to answer.

The belief that a human life is worth that of many sparrows is widely acted on. The problem here is that the worth of the sparrow is too often altogether neglected or even denied. But in the wider sphere, there are serious divisions among those who agree that the care of the earth involves responsible concern for other species as well. One group emphasizes that we should reduce the amount of suffering we inflict on individual animals. Another group focuses attention on the health of the biosphere as a whole and on the importance of maintaining diversity of species in healthy interrelatedness. For them, micro-organisms and insects may be more important to preserve than whales and chimpanzees. The former group values creatures intrinsically according to their capacity for suffering and enjoyment. The latter group values them instrumentally for their contribution to the ecosystem.

From the perspective established in the first chapter of Genesis, both concerns are warranted. Each creature is good in itself and good for God. For any creature to suffer unnecessarily is an evil, and since it is reasonable to believe that whales and chimpanzees are subject to far more suffering than fish and beetles, concern to decrease the suffering inflicted by human beings is rightly directed more to the former than to the latter. But it would be possible to greatly reduce this suffering while human actions destroy the remaining tropical forests, habitat for the majority of species of living things on this planet. This loss of biodiversity impoverishes the earth in fundamental ways. The body of God can become sick. It may cease, in God's perception as well, to be very good. Eventually, human beings may be one of the species for whom the earth no longer provides habitat.

Indeed, care of the earth must direct itself beyond the sphere of living things. They contribute to the chemical balance of the earth, but if this balance is changed too much by human activity, living things will not be able to adjust. Chemical poisoning on a local scale is already widespread, and we are realizing that human activity has changed the chemistry of the global environment as well, so that the ozone layer and planetary weather patterns are affected. These may be only examples of a wide range of chemical imbalances with which our descendants must contend as a result of our activity. No care of the earth that neglects these fundamental requirements for healthy life can be adequate.

Most of the human activity that injures other creatures and threatens the health of the earth is economic. There can be no genuine care of the earth that does not impinge radically on economics. Thus far, this point has been neglected. Of course, there are laws against specific economic practices that directly pollute air and water. A few regions have been identified as wilderness and placed off limits to economic exploitation, at least for the time being. International efforts are being made to restrict economic activities that degrade the ozone layer. But the goals of national and international economic development still include endless increase of the industrialization of the planet. It is argued that only economic prosperity provides the wealth needed to deal with environmental issues, and that only ever-increasing industrialization produces the needed wealth.

This pervasive self-delusion underlying almost all current policies renders our talk of care for the earth largely empty. While we use bandages to deal with scratches, we are engaged in breaking bones. Until those concerned with the earth can at least propose a positive alternative scenario, prospects for the earth remain bleak indeed.

Around the fringes of contemporary thought, proposals are emerging. New farming methods—and some very ancient ones—are being developed that do not degrade the soil or depend on petroleum-based inputs. Reduced consumption of meat in industrial countries would ease pressure on fuel and on the land itself, as well as improve health. Return to primary dependence on locally grown produce could lead both to more nutritious food and to reduced energy use in transportation.

Paolo Soleri has shown how human habitat could be designed to free land for other uses. It could also be powered chiefly by solar energy so as to leave remaining oil supplies for other needs. And it could eliminate the need for automotive transportation within cities.

Such changes would *reduce* the gross national product but *improve* human welfare. This fact dramatizes the distortions introduced into current policies by commitments to increase production. Even today, there is little correlation between the amount of product and the level of human well-being. Economic policies need to be redesigned to serve human well-being rather than increase of product.

One main way in which the economy has worked against human well-being has been through its indifference to community. It has conceived human beings as individual consumers of goods and services so that greater consumption is conceived as greater well-being. The increase of production has required increased specialization, larger markets, and mobility of labor and capital. All of these are attained at the expense of breaking up traditional communities and, again and again, new communities formed around new economies. This repeated assault on community has enormous psychological, social, and political effects. Realizing this, some countries have subordinated the economy to community concerns and held these consequences in check. But in our country, the economy is primary and society is left to cope with the human devastation it generates. We cannot care for the earth without subordinating the economy to the needs of the human community.

This call is likely to be heard among market enthusiasts as an appeal for socialism. It is not. In its Marxist forms, at least, socialism has been even more ruthless than capitalism in its assault on human community. The *Homo economicus* of socialist theory is as far removed from a communal view of the human person as is the *Homo economicus* of standard Western economics. Of course, both systems can contribute elements to an economics for community.

When human beings understand themselves as part of a wider community, the earth that God saw to be very good, then the inadequacy and inappropriateness of both capitalism and socialism become even clearer. Neither has viewed creation as a unity that includes human beings. Both treat all that is not human as mere means to human ends. An economy designed to serve the whole creaturely community, the body of God, would be very different indeed from either capitalism or socialism.

To care for the earth is to care for the whole community of creatures that together make up this planet. Some have felt that this inclusive caring works against concern for the poor and oppressed and, indeed, some of those concerned about other species of living things and about the long-term future seem to be ready to sacrifice the immediate need for justice. Those who refuse to make comparative judgments as to the value of diverse creatures in themselves and for God sometimes also disparage ethical concerns about human social relations. But on the whole, this antithesis has ben exaggerated. Most of those concerned for the other living things with which we share the planet are also keenly concerned for the members of our own species. Most of those who want to extend ethical considerations to other creatures think ethically about human relations as well. The care of the earth is indivisible, and those with different emphases should not allow themselves to be divided and conquered by the exploiters of both the human poor and the nonhuman creatures.

On the whole, those least sensitive to the consequences of human actions for plants and animals and for the general health of the environment also have been least sensitive to the well-being of the people whose livelihood is most immediately dependent on that world: the hunters and gatherers, the nomads, the subsistence farmers, and the traditional fisherfolk. They have "developed" the economies in ways that have benefited the rich and powerful at the expense of the poor and powerless. It is the poor and powerless who suffer most as resources are exhausted and pollution increases. Too often the poor and powerless, especially when they are culturally and ethnically different, are treated as part of the resources for development rather than as subjects of development. Usually, the interests of defenseless people and of a defenseless environment coincide. The care of the earth is the care of the whole human community as a part of the larger community. If it neglects the larger community, it will fail.

Both "economies" and "ecology" refer in their root meanings to the care of the *ecos*, the household. The Greek household of New Testament times was often a sizable unit of production as well as consumption, providing intimate community as well as security for all its members. Care of the household dealt both with the management of its internal life and with its relations to other households and the *polis*. In the modern world, the household has become the nuclear family or the individual human being. In economics, the individual has become the model for considering households, so that relations among family members are not discussed. Only the relations to others are viewed as important, and among these, only those that follow market patterns. "Ecology," on the other hand, has expanded the *ecos* so that the household to which care is directed is the whole earth. The implication of seeing the world as God's creation is that we should be guided by modern ecology rather than modern economics in ordering our human activity.

In the beginning, in every beginning, God was creating, and in the continuation, in every continuation, God continues to create. God is everlasting creator, and there is no beginning or ending to God's creative activity. Human beings created in God's image, can participate consciously and intentionally in the work of creation. In many ways, we have done so, enriching the earth. But in many and appalling ways, we have turned our creative powers against God's purposes for the whole of creation. Claiming that in all creation God cares only for us—or claiming, still more extravagantly, that we are in fact the only creators—we have imposed our narrow and short-term goals upon the earth. We are already paying a high price for our sin. But if we continue, the price will be much higher, perhaps our extinction. The question is whether this escalating price will evoke repentance before it is too late.